PERSECUTION COMPLEX

Why American Christians Need to Stop
Playing the Victim

By Jason Wiedel

Persecution Complex
Why American Christians Need to Stop Playing the Victim

CrowdScribed
2575 Kelley Point Parkway, Suite 360, Edmond, OK 73013

Published in the United States by CrowdScribed, LLC

Library of Congress Cataloging-in-Publication Data
Library of Congress Control Number: 2014950620

Typeset by CrowdScribed in conjunction with Lightning Source, La Vergne, Tennessee

Printed in the United States by Lightning Source on acid-free paper
Book design by Brianna Spayd

Cover Image © Can Stock Photo Inc/Jason Wiedel
All interior images are public domain.

ISBN 978-0-9905917-4-0

PERSECUTION COMPLEX

Why American Christians Need to
Stop Playing the Victim

by Jason Wiedel

PERSECUTION COMPLEX
-The Book-

"In this insightful book, Jason reveals how the perception of persecution amongst American Evangelicals is not just false, it's destructive--the very antithesis of the gospel Evangelicals supposedly proclaim. Better yet, he offers some key steps on how Christians can abandon the victim narrative in favor of a script that offers them a much better role: positive agents of change in this world."

--**Kevin Miller**, director of "Hellbound?"

"Once in a while I read a book I wish I'd written. This is one such book. 'Important' hardly covers it. To understand the madness that has embittered paranoid American religion into a thoroughly delusional and dangerous movement, read this book!"

--**Frank Schaeffer,** author of *Why I Am an Atheist Who Believes in God.*

"Jason Wiedel cuts through the fog around this issue and reveals the truth behind the persecution complex: we're not being persecuted, we're losing privilege. Wiedel's insights and exploration in to this concept help us to see why the loss of privilege is actually a blessing and how the false narrative of persecution is damaging Christianity and our witness to the world. This book is a difficult read for American Christians, but one that must be read and examined carefully. I believe that hope for a brighter future lie within these pages and I am convinced that everyone who reads this book with a posture of humility will be challenged, refined, and blessed by Wiedel's message."

--**Brandan Robertson**, *Revangelical*

Contents

Acknowledgements

Thanks to everyone who voted for this book and helped make it a reality. Thank you especially to my wife, Della, and my mother, Carol, for your encouragement, ideas, and editing. Thanks to Brandon Robertson for your input, especially regarding the topic of justice. Thank you, Frank Schaeffer, for your creative input.

Thanks also to Kevin Miller, Michael Hardin, Steve Hansen, and Christian Piatt for your encouragement and commitment to communicating what Christianity should really look like.

Introduction

In March 2014, the film *God's Not Dead* was a surprise box office hit, grossing $9.2 million on its opening weekend and earning nearly $70 million as of the writing of this book. *Variety* called it "the biggest shocker" of the weekend. The success of this movie should not have come as a surprise, though. *God's Not Dead* was enormously popular with one audience in particular: Evangelical Christians. Why? Because it perfectly captures the persecution narrative that has become the central worldview of so many Christians in America.

God's Not Dead tells the story of a college student named Josh whose faith is challenged by his atheist philosophy professor. Josh must prove the existence of God or fail his philosophy class. Many film critics found this premise to be ridiculous. That is not the point though. The filmmakers wanted their Christian audience to identify with Josh, who stands up for his faith despite severe criticism. The movie wants us to see the secular world as a source of anti-Christian persecution. The film also wants us to take up the call to battle these forces of secularism that are seeking to eliminate Christianity from the public sphere.

The ridiculous part of *God's Not Dead* is not the professor's pass/fail challenge. It is the creation of a world where atheists are pitted against theists and non-Christians against Christians in a battle for the soul of our culture. *God's Not Dead* creates a simplistic, dualistic world, where one is either in or out, and the ones who are in are always the good guys. They are always us.

The film portrays not only atheists but also Muslims, academics, and wealthy business people as persecutors of Christians. (In fact, the film's only positively portrayed characters are church-going Christians, the Newsboys, and the stars of *Duck Dynasty*.) *God's Not Dead* communicates the idea that the highest vocation of the Christian is to stand up for Christ amidst the onslaught of daily persecution.

Persecuting Young People

When I was in high school, I was part of a youth ministry in a non-denominational, Evangelical church. We had meetings every Sunday night where we played games, listened to a Bible lesson, and ate Oreo cookies.

One evening when we gathered, our leaders told us we were going on an outing. We climbed into the church van, where we had to don blindfolds. After a short drive, we piled out of the van and found ourselves in an old barn lit by a dim gas lantern.

One of the leaders proceeded to read a newspaper article informing us that Christian gatherings were now illegal and that pastors who attempted to assemble their churches would be arrested. This was the reason for the blindfolds and the secret location. Then we found a comfortable place in the loft of the barn and proceeded to pray and conduct our illegal youth meeting.

It was a pleasant evening in the old barn—until we were interrupted by flashing blue lights and a police siren. Our youth pastor went out to investigate. He was promptly handcuffed and taken away in the police car.

Of course, the entire evening was an elaborate object lesson. (It was fairly effective though, since it is one of the few lessons I remember from my years in youth group.) Our adventure was crafted to reveal how Christians are forced to function in places where they are persecuted and to warn us what life would be like if Christian persecution ever came to the United States. While our leaders were not intentionally trying to instill fear in us, they were promoting the idea that persecution is a very real problem against which we should be prepared to fight.

Growing up in the Evangelical world, this idea was continually reinforced. I heard it in Sunday school and in Sunday morning preaching. I heard it in the Christian music to which I listened, saw it in Christian movies, and read about it in Christian books. I learned that those who worked to remove prayer from public schools were not following a constitutional mandate of separation of church and state or considering the diverse beliefs of all Americans but were secularists (hell-) bent on the destruction of one faith only: Christianity. Those who supported legalized abortion were not validating the rights of women to control their own reproduction but were murderers determined to eliminate millions of "inconvenient" children. Those who mocked Christians didn't do so because they had had bad experiences with rude, obnoxious, and selfish believers; they were opposed to the love of Jesus, perhaps even as part of some broad, Satanic conspiracy.

In response, at youth group, youth conferences, and in ministry training, I was taught continually to stand up for my faith. Over time, I came to realize that one of the highest values of the Evangelical world is to stand up for one's faith.

The idea of Christians as an excluded "other" has deep roots in America's history. Our Puritan forbearers left Europe to escape persecution from state churches. Separatists, Quakers, Anabaptists, Catholics, and many others came to America for the promise of religious liberty.

Fast forward to the present, where a culture war is being fought to identify the "true believers" and determine whose values will control American society. Many American Evangelicals imagine themselves engaged in a battle for the country's soul, not only with secularists but also with progressive and liberal Christians, whom they regard as nothing more than wolves in sheep's clothing.

It's a Myth

While the notion of a culture war has been used primarily by political ideologues to rally their troops, it has also caused many evangelicals to see religious persecution under every rock. The Ten Commandments are removed from the courthouse lobby? Religious persecution. The opening prayer at an event is replaced by a moment of silence? Persecution. Teachers are prohibited from wearing religious T-shirts to school? Persecution. The cashier wishes you

"Happy Holidays" instead of "Merry Christmas"? Persecution, persecution, persecution.

We have a persecution complex. An obsession.

I worked in church ministry for nearly 20 years. During that time, I interacted almost exclusively with people who were part of the religious institution. Over the past ten years or so, I have come to know more people who reside outside the bounds of conservative Evangelical Christianity— atheists, liberals, homosexuals, scientists, educators, philosophers, and those who identify with other religions—people who I might once have considered my enemies. The thing is, when you get to know your enemy, the conflict and contention begins to disappear. This is exactly what happened to me. I came to realize that my years of entrenchment in the narrative of persecution had deprived me of relationships with amazing people, positive developmental experiences, and a truer understanding of God's character.

I now believe that Christians in America are not persecuted or oppressed. I will go so far as to say the persecution of American Christians is a myth, a fiction that serves to bind many American Evangelical communities together. It is a legitimizing force for our religious activities, a motivator for evangelism, and an excuse to behave badly toward those with whom we disagree. Worst of all, it distracts us from the real problems of human suffering, to which Jesus instructed his followers to attend. What many Christians perceive as persecution is actually fear of losing their privileged place in society, a fear that is exploited by the very people who have the most to lose from this shift in status.

In this book, I look at how the persecution myth developed amongst American Evangelicals, what makes it so attractive, and how we can go about writing a new script regarding our place in society.

My hope is that by telling this story, I will encourage American Evangelicals to reconsider their role in the culture and work toward developing truly loving relationships with secularists, other believers, and those groups in America and abroad who are suffering from real persecution and injustice. Seeing as the persecution narrative has created so much bad blood between Evangelicals and their neighbors, I also hope this book will give outsiders a better understanding of how the Evangelical mind works as a foundation for future dialogue and reconciliation.

PART 1

What is the Persecution Narrative?

1

The American Christian Persecution Narrative: A Definition

The film *Back to the Future* is a prime example of the dominant cultural script of the 1980s. In the film, Michael J. Fox plays Marty McFly, who accidentally travels back in time to 1955. In the process, he accidentally causes the teenage version of his mother to fall in love with him, which creates the potential of erasing his own future existence if he can't get his teenage parents to fall in love on the very same night they got together in his current timeline.

Back to the Future is full of the cultural themes that dominated much of the 1980s: teenage heroes, clueless adult authorities, weak females, well-intentioned but ultimately dangerous technology, and materialism. Numerous other movies from that decade feature these similar themes: *Ferris Bueller's Day Off, The Breakfast Club, E.T., Pretty in Pink, Footloose...*

Every generation, decade, geographic location, and subculture follows a script. Films of the

1980s contain similar themes, because this was the script that was structuring the lives of American young people at the time. Cultural scripts are made up of the values and influences of a particular group that happens to dominate the society. A script is the narrative that is both controlling and being directed by this group.

In the 1980s, the United States experienced economic expansion. Reaganomics was credited for giving us cheap gas, rising wages, business growth, and low-cost goods. Material success became an important value in America. The end of *Back to the Future* clearly expresses this value as Marty McFly finds that when he returns to the present, his father has a good job, his family has lots of nice things, and he has a shiny new truck waiting for him in the garage. They all live happily ever after with wealth and material possessions (until *Back to the Future 2*).

When Marty McFly goes back to the 1950s, the cultural script that controlled much of America was the defense of the American way of life against communism. American citizens put up with the tactics of J. Edgar Hoover and Joseph McCarthy, because the dominant narrative told them the evils of communism were America's greatest threat. This narrative made patriotism

Americans' most important value and justified any action taken by the United States government.

With the cultural revolution of the 1960s, the Vietnam War, and the Watergate scandal, the cultural script changed. Unquestioning patriotism was replaced by suspicion of politicians and government. Not surprisingly, film, television, and literature reflected this change. Movies like *Dirty Harry*, *Taxi Driver*, and *Network* encouraged Americans to question authority and gave them a more pessimistic view of the world.

The Script of Persecution

Although the broader culture tends to have a dominant script, so does every subculture. American evangelicals are no different. Their script is called *the persecution narrative*, and it goes something like this...

God has given us specific commands in Scripture. We honor him by obeying these commands. When we obey God, we find his way is the best way to live. God loves and cares for humanity, and living outside his will results in a dysfunctional and unhealthy life.

America is moving increasingly further from the will of God. This is evidenced by the endorsement of pluralism and moral relativism, blatant immorality,

> If you are going to walk with Jesus Christ, you are going to be opposed ... In our days, to be a true Christian is really to become a scandal.
>
> —George Whitefield

the growing embrace of homosexuality, the increasing acceptance of sex outside of marriage, the large number of abortions performed every year, the dysfunction of families, the disrespect and violence from young people, and the priority of issues such as environmentalism and animal rights above the well-being of humans. Christians are called to point out the way these evils are creeping into society. As people drift further from God, however, they are not responsive to his commands. They become hostile and attempt to silence the voices that point out their rebellion.

These anti-Christian forces have been successful in removing prayer from public schools and legalizing abortion in America. Now they are hard at work attempting to remove all traces of Christianity from public life. These are the people who sue public institutions, forcing them to remove displays of the Ten Commandments or the Bible. They want "In God We Trust" removed from our currency and "Under God" taken out of the Pledge of Allegiance. They are patrolling public schools and military installations looking for displays of Christianity to attack. They are working within our government, attempting to limit religious freedom and undermine the position of Christianity in American life. They are also working from within; seeking to water down Christianity so no one will be offended by its claims or requirements.

Our enemies also want us to forget our Christian heritage, the founders who based this nation's laws and governmental structure on Christian morals and principles. They vilify the heroes of the past by exaggerating their involvement in slavery, the genocide of Native Americans, American imperialism, and individual founders' personal moral failings. In short, they want to deny the greatness of America's Christian past and its exceptionality as a nation.

Happy is the nation whose God is the LORD, the people whom he has chosen as his heritage.

Psalm 33:12

In the present, they want to distract us from truly important spiritual and moral issues by focusing society's attention on climate change, scientific research, civil rights, income inequality, prison reform, drug legalization, education, gender equality, and universal health care.

They also want to marginalize Christians as much as possible, excluding us from public discourse by claiming we are intolerant, minimizing the Church's influence in society, and making us the subject of mockery in the media.

All of this amounts to an organized effort to persecute Christians in America. Some Christians do not recognize this persecution. They are asleep. Those of us who do recognize the persecution must stand against it. Standing against persecution can take many forms: speaking out against the blatantly anti-Christian efforts of secularists, protesting laws that limit religious freedom, voting for those who will uphold the Christian heritage of this nation, and speaking loudly and clearly about the dangers of immorality.

Christians are being repressed, persecuted. We must take action.

The persecution narrative says Christians are the underdogs being attacked by the combined forces of atheists, liberals, socialists, and multiculturalists. It tells us we are in danger from the gay agenda, the liberal agenda, and the militant Muslim agenda. The persecution narrative conflates Christianity with American ideals, convincing us that patriotism is a Christian virtue. Therefore, in addition to attacks on our faith, we should also fear gun control, illegal immigration, and government-mandated healthcare. In this effort to win back the culture, the government is seen as both our greatest ally and our worst enemy. It tells us that our best days are behind us, and we should fear the future, fighting for a return to the cultural values of the 1950s, or perhaps even the 1770s.

The Persecution Complex

Persecutory delusion is a physiological condition characterized by a perception that someone is

PERSECUTION IS NOT . . .

When prayer is removed from schools

When Bible verses are removed from public places

When comedians make fun of Christians

When prayer meetings are not allowed in public places

When cashiers say "Happy Holidays"

When college groups are required to be inclusive of gay people

When religious events include various religions

When homeowner's associations will not let churches meet in their neighborhood attempting to harm the afflicted individual. This condition is often associated with schizophrenia. The DSM-IV-TR (Diagnostic and Statistical Manual of Mental Disorders) describes a person suffering from persecutory delusion as believing "he or she is being tormented, followed, tricked, spied on, or ridiculed."

The story of John Nash is told in the film *A Beautiful Mind*. Nash was a brilliant mathematician whose theories have been used in a wide range of disciplines, including economics, evolutionary biology, and artificial intelligence. In 1994, he received a Nobel Prize in economic sciences. Despite his brilliance, at times Nash believed people were secretly plotting against and persecuting him. That's because Nash struggled with mental illness, including paranoid schizophrenia.

When baptisms are not allowed in public parks

When television networks remove religious content

When employees are asked not to wear Christian messages

When people refuse to support a business whose owners refuse to support gay marriage

When businesses are forced to serve everyone, even people with whom they disagree

Unlike many people who suffer from such afflictions, Nash was able to overcome his delusions. He states in his autobiography, "Then gradually I began to intellectually reject some of the delusionally influenced lines of thinking which had been characteristic of my orientation."[1] Although Nash's incredible mental ability enabled him to overcome his mental illness, for many people, schizophrenia, persecutory delusion, and paranoia are terribly debilitating.

9

I do not wish to characterize American Evangelicals as clinically delusional. However, I do believe that what many American Evangelicals regard as persecution is similar to symptoms experienced by people afflicted with this mental disorder.

No man is happy without a delusion of some kind. Delusions are as necessary to our happiness as realities.

—C. N. Bovee

As I have mentioned, in many circles of Christianity, the idea that we are a persecuted minority is continually reinforced in children's lessons, teen curriculums, novels, movies, Sunday sermons, and so on. For some, the assumption of persecution is as much a part of the Christian life as baptism and the Bible. Well-known pastor John Piper wrote, "Once upon a time, there was a safe, private place to take your controversial stand for Jesus. No more. If you are going to stand, you will be shot at—either figuratively or literally."[2]

Viewing ourselves as the persecuted minority is ironic, because much of the broader culture sees Christians, especially conservative Evangelicals, as the oppressive majority. A report published by People for the American Way in May 2014 addresses the issues of religious persecution. The conclusion of this report says, "Religious freedom is a core constitutional value and a cornerstone of our liberty. But the Religious Right's narrative of religious persecution is not only far from the truth; in many cases the narrative itself serves to undermine true religious liberty and individual freedom for all."[3]

In many cases the perception of American Christians regarding persecution is completely out of line with the cultural reality. We have embraced a delusion— the persecution complex.

What If We Are Wrong?

The persecution narrative can only exist in an environment of pride, because, it is completely self-centered. It takes hold when Christians insist they fully understand the truth and believe it is their responsibility to defend that truth. The persecution narrative loses its grip, however, when Christians embrace humility and place the needs of others above their own.

Embracing humility means admitting we might be wrong. It means having more confidence in God and less confidence in ourselves. It means admitting that sometimes we get things wrong when we try to understand God's heart and carry out God's will. It means holding our doctrine loosely while holding tightly to Jesus.

Rather than inciting us to humility, the persecution narrative incites pride, fear, and selfishness. It causes us to cling tightly to particular beliefs, because if we lose them, we fear we'll lose the culture. If we can begin to loosen our grip, accept that we might be wrong about some things, and then enter into dialogue on these points, then the delusion of the persecution complex also begins to loosen its hold on us.

More Examples of Cultural Scripts in Film

1980s—Might Makes Right
- *First Blood*
- *Escape From New York*
- *Predator*
- *Big Trouble in Little China*
- *Raiders of the Lost Ark*
- *Commando*
- *Terminator*
- *The Delta Force*

2000s—Reality Is Not Real
- *The Matrix*
- *The 13th Floor*
- *Equilibrium*
- *Dark City*
- *Minority Report*
- *Memento*
- *Vanilla Sky*
- *The Truman Show*

2010s—Teens Save Society
- *The Hunger Games*
- *Divergent*
- *Maze Runner*
- *The Giver*
- *Percy Jackson*
- *Ender's Game*
- *The Seeker*
- *The 100* (TV)
- *Tomorrow People* (TV)

Summer of the Shark

Summer 2001 was dominated by news of shark attacks. The July 30 issue of *Time* declared it the "Summer of the Shark." Local and national news stories described shark attacks and sightings taking place on both the East Coast and the West Coast. One might think sharks had suddenly become more numerous, more aggressive, or developed a new taste for human flesh. The reality, though, was that shark attacks were no more proliferate during the summer of 2001 than at any other time.

It was the story of eight-year-old Jessie Arbogast, who was mauled by a bull shark while wading in knee-deep water near Pensacola at the beginning of July, that sparked a national interest in shark attacks. Sharks became a part of the cultural narrative. The public was interested, so the media reported on sharks, so the public became more interested. The feedback loop created by the media maintained and perpetuated the narrative that was driving society at any given time. We see this happen over and over again with various issues, such as the current fears about Ebola.

Reports of shark attacks would likely not have captured the attention of Americans in the middle of the Dust Bowl or during World War II.

Sharks were not a part of the cultural narrative during those times, but in 2001, stories of sharks created a script that captivated America.

Until September...

When planes crashed into the World Trade Center, the Pentagon, and a Western Pennsylvania field on September 11 of that year, America forgot all about sharks. The script changed suddenly and drastically. Our collective fear shifted to terrorism and Muslims, and the media would not be reporting on shark epidemics for many years.

As mentioned, cultural scripts can include a large segment of society or a relatively small segment. In either case, they become the lens through which we see much of the world. It influences the news to which we pay attention, the issues that are important to us, and the media we consume. The Christian persecution narrative has done fulfilled all of these functions for American Evangelicals for about twenty years.

Films like *God's Not Dead* can seem nonsensical or even offensive to some people,[4] but these films fit perfectly into the persecution narrative, so they are celebrated by those living out the persecution script. "Finally, a movie that reflects our values." Warnings of the loss of religious liberty can seem like gross exaggeration to many people, but since these stories fit neatly into the persecution narrative, they are welcomed by those who live within that script.

Embrace of the persecution narrative is not a simple matter. It is not just an opinion a person forms about a single issue. It is a worldview, and just like America's 2001 obsession with sharks, it makes perfect sense when we are immersed in it. It only begins to look untrue when we gain some distance from it.

Rewriting the Script

Abandoning the script and adopting a new narrative to explain our place in the world can be both painful and terrifying. It can result in a loss of relationships, changes in our political views, a reassessment of our values, and a horrible feeling of instability as we look for new footing. However, if we want to be authentic, effective followers of Jesus, I believe we must reject the persecution narrative. I will not pretend this is an easy process. It is an uncomfortable journey that we must take one step at a time.

To facilitate this process, we need to understand where this narrative came from exactly and why we find it so attractive. We will turn to these topics next.

2

Where Did the Christian Persecution Narrative Come From?

"Blessed are you when people revile you and persecute you and utter all kinds of evil against you falsely on my account. Rejoice and be glad, for your reward is great in heaven, for in the same way they persecuted the prophets who were before you" (Matthew 5:11–12).

Biblical Roots

Ironically, our understanding of anti-Christian persecution has its foundation in Scripture. The gospels record several instances when Jesus warns his followers that they will be persecuted, but he encourages them to embrace this persecution with the confidence that they are on the right path. The early Church embraced suffering and martyrdom as important ways to identify with Christ.

Early Christians faced severe persecution, first from their Jewish neighbors and then from the wider Roman world. The values of Christ came into conflict with the Jewish system of religion

And everyone who has left houses or brothers or sisters or father or mother or children or fields, for my name's sake, will receive a hundredfold, and will inherit eternal life.

Matthew 19:29

and with the system of empire. When one system threatens another, conflict always ensues.

When we read the Bible, we should remember that most of it was written in a context of oppression, where the authors were exiled, captive, marginalized, or oppressed. As American Christians, we have a position of wealth, privilege, and power. This is about as different as can be from the position of the first-century Christians who first read the gospels and the New Testament epistles.

> For those who want to save their life will lose it, and those who lose their life for my sake will save it.
>
> Luke 9:24

When Emperor Constantine brought the Roman Empire under the banner of the cross, Christianity suddenly became the religion of the majority and the privileged. Since that time, although Christians have endured persecution in places where Christianity has not been the dominant religion—such as the Middle East, the Soviet Union, China, and North Korea—Christians have faced almost no organized persecution in the Western world.

We do see conflicts between Christians that result in communities being targeted based on their religion. Violent conflicts in places like Northern Ireland, Somalia, Croatia, and Rwanda have targeted Christians, but we should be careful not to characterize these as anti-Christian persecution. In many conflicts, Christian groups have been just as guilty of perpetuating violence as other religious groups. Most of these clashes should be placed in the category of civil war, not religious persecution.

There are instances where Christians have been marginalized and abused in America. Although it is not common, it does happen. However, I believe that we should be slow to claim persecution for our religious beliefs. Many factors contribute to mistreatment. Often a person or group is simply looking for an excuse to mistreat another person. Many times Christians have been identified and targeted for characteristics that should not be attributed to followers of Jesus. Are Christians persecuted because they embrace Christ or because of behavior that does not honor Christ? Oswald Chambers puts this tension brilliantly:

> At heart men are antagonistic to the lordship of Jesus Christ. It is not antagonism to creeds or points of view, but antagonism encountered for My sake. Many of us awaken antagonism by our way of stating things; we have to distinguish between being persecuted for some notion of our own and being persecuted "for My sake."[5]

Jesus said, "Truly I tell you, there is no one who has left house or brothers or sisters or mother or father or children or fields, for my sake and for the sake of the good news, who will not receive a hundredfold now in this age—houses, brothers and sisters, mothers and children, and fields, with persecutions— and in the age to come eternal life.

Mark 10:29–30

19

Ancient Values

Some anthropologists assert that many of the values the Western world embraces today have roots in the teachings and life of Jesus. In his book *Humilitas*, biblical scholar John Dickson asserts that the modern idea that humility is a virtue grew directly from the example of Jesus' death. Dickson explains that in antiquity, humility was not the sign of moral character it is today.

Ancient Greeks and Romans thought nothing of praising themselves in public or, better still, getting others to praise them. No one appreciated crass boasting or boasting that put others down—hubris or arrogance. Nor was self-love advisable, as the Greek myth of Narcissus falling in love with his reflection teaches. But taking hold of the honour due to your merit was perfectly acceptable. It was taken for granted that those with merit would seek the honour due to them.

Dickson goes on to describe how his work in an academic research project at Macquarie University led to the conclusion that the life of Jesus Christ is responsible for our current view of humility.

It took a couple of centuries for this to catch on throughout the Roman/Western world, but once it did, it became commonplace for people, whether or not they were Christians, to use the once negative words *humilitas* and the Greek equivalent *tapeinos* in the positive sense of deliberately lowering yourself for the good of others—namely, humility.[6]

It is likely that persecution and martyrdom have followed the same course of development that humility has taken. As Christianity has helped shape Western culture over the past centuries, the idea that enduring persecution is virtuous and that persecution validates our activities and beliefs has become a dominant theme.

Jesus' endorsement of persecution is no longer exclusively for his followers. Nearly every cause or movement sees persecution as a confirmation of their moral standing, even if they do not identify with Jesus. Everyone wants to be a victim, because everyone assumes victims occupy the moral high ground.

The general, moral ethos of persecution gives credence to most causes, but Christians can also look to the specific words of Jesus for validation. We can feel that we are following Jesus more closely when we can apply his words about persecution directly to our situation.

"Of course they are opposing us. Jesus said the world would hate us. Jesus said we would be persecuted for his sake." This is the kind of language one hears in many churches across America. Persecution is attractive to Christians. It gives legitimacy to our cause. It identifies us with Jesus. It fulfills the words of Scripture. And it shows us that the return of Jesus is imminent.

Hijacking the Book of Revelation

CE stands for Common Era. This term has replaced AD, meaning Anno Domini, which is Latin for "in the year of our Lord." Some people have identified the use of CE as another example of the repression of Christianity and the removal of anything related to Jesus from the social consciousness. The term Common Era can actually

The book of Revelation was written around 90CE (see sidebar) by a man named John who was exiled to the island of Patmos. According to many scholars, this was likely not John the apostle of Jesus but a Christian named John who is not identified in any other part of the Bible.

The book of Revelation is a critique of the first-century Roman Empire written in a style called *apocalyptic*. Apocalyptic does not refer to the end of the world but to a revelation or unveiling of a hidden message. John's writing is a coded message that reveals the spiritual conflict between the kingdom of God and the kingdom of Rome. In Revelation, John reveals the corruption of Rome and tells first century Christians how they should relate to the empire in which they live.

Rather than export this critique of empire to our modern context, many American Evangelicals have come to see Revelation as a prediction of the end of the world, when Christians will be vindicated and the enemies of God will be punished. Many of us assume that Revelation has always been understood this way. But this perspective did not gain traction until the 1800s with the writings of John Nelson Darby of the Plymouth Brethren. And it was not until the publishing of Hal Lindsey's *The Late Great Planet Earth* in 1970 that this end-of-the-world interpretation of Revelation became widely understood and accepted by American Evangelicals. Lindsey, followed by other evangelists, authors, and filmmakers, popularized the idea that we are living in the end times and Jesus could return at any moment.

be traced to as far back as 1615. The use of the term CE has become standard because it does not prefer a Eurocentric view of history.

The book of Revelation is often cited, in conjunction with Jesus' words in Matthew 24, as a prediction of the end-times persecution of Christians:

> Then they will hand you over to be tortured and will put you to death, and you will be hated by all nations because of my name. Then many will fall away, and they will betray one another and hate one another. And many false prophets will arise and lead many astray. And because of the increase of lawlessness, the love of many will grow

23

cold. But the one who endures to the end will be saved. And this good news of the kingdom will be proclaimed throughout the world, as a testimony to all the nations; and then the end will come. (v. 9–14)

"Saint Michael Trampling the Dragon"
by Raphael Sanzio, 1518

Perhaps part of Jesus and John's predictions was about events that would take place thousands of years in the future. We must remember though, that they were writing and speaking to those who lived in the Middle East in the first century. They were addressing the persecution experienced by those early followers of Jesus, explaining to those early Christians what it meant to live in the kingdom of God while in captivity, exile, and under the thumb of empire.

When we view Revelation only or primarily as a description of the end times, it becomes about a violent and vengeful God who does not resemble Jesus of Nazareth at all. It becomes not a revelation of Jesus Christ, as the first verse of Revelation asserts, but the return to a god of violent, retributive judgment. This misreading of Revelation is a major contributor to so many problematic positions in Evangelical Christianity: refusal to address environmental problems, opposition to globalism, support for war against Muslim nations, unquestioning support of Israel, a willingness to use military violence to solve international conflicts rather than seeking peaceful solutions, and most egregiously, the embrace of a violent and vengeful god.

This same end time theology leads to a particular view of persecution. Those whose belief about the end of the world resembles the *Left Behind* novels assume that anti-Christian persecution is a signal that the end is near. The worse it gets, the closer we are to that day. Believing we are persecuted for Jesus' sake affirms to us that we are on the path of righteousness, identifies us with Jesus, and gives us the confidence that Jesus will return soon to punish the wicked and reward us for standing firm. Therefore, rather than serving as positive, constructive agents in the world, all we need to do is hunker down and hold out until the end.

Fundamentalism

Christian fundamentalism emerged in the late nineteenth century. Reacting to the emergence of historical criticism in biblical scholarship, evolutionary theory, and social gospel teaching, Fundamentalists sought to hold on to the "fundamentals" of Christianity, which they saw being undermined by the broader culture and watered down by liberal theology. This movement primarily involved conservative Presbyterians and Baptists.

Fundamentalists are traditionally regarded as Christians who accept biblical inerrancy, the Virgin birth, the divinity of Jesus, substitutionary atonement, the literal resurrection of Jesus, and the second coming of Christ. However, in recent years, the word *fundamentalist* has come to connote any person who holds to rigid, exclusivist beliefs. We have fundamentalist Muslims, fundamentalist Jews, and even fundamentalist atheists, anyone who has an extreme and often irrational commitment to a particular perspective. In the past we might have used the terms *dogmatic* or *foundationalist* to describe the person we now call a fundamentalist.

Fundamentalism developed in conjunction with the dispensationalist views of John Nelson Darby. This resulted in a majority of Fundamentalists having a pessimistic eschatology. Pessimistic eschatology is the belief that the world is becoming progressively worse, and Jesus must return to rescue his people prior to the destruction at the end of days. This perspective has seeped into nearly every form of Christianity in America over the past 100 years.

The development of Christian fundamentalism was a reaction to what the early Fundamentalists considered attacks on Christianity. New methods of scholarship, archeological discovery, and scientific research produced ideas that were contrary to what many Christians held to be true. As evolutionary theory became more widely accepted in the late 1800s, many church leaders became afraid that the truth of Scripture was being threatened.

The emergence of evolutionary theory also coincided with a widespread acceptance of historical critical biblical scholarship. Historical criticism examines the Bible in light of history and anthropology. This kind of examination of the Bible began to move scholars away from a literalistic approach to the Bible, which many Evangelicals consider the hallmark of genuine Christianity.

Fundamentalists continued to stand against issues that they assumed would lead to cultural deterioration. Many Fundamentalists opposed the teaching of evolution in public schools, supported prohibition, opposed desegregation, and supported prayer and Bible reading in public schools. Many Fundamentalists also become quite excited by the formation of the state of Israel in 1948, assuming that this was the first step in events that would lead to the return of Christ.

Christian fundamentalism has affected almost all expressions of Christianity in America and has laid the foundation for today's persecution complex.

Fear of Communism and Fear of Persecution

The most shocking World War II propaganda poster I have seen portrays Jesus on the cross being shot at by Hitler and Mussolini. Another poster from this period shows a Nazi soldier stabbing a knife through a Bible. Not only were fascists and Nazis portrayed as enemies of America, it seems they were also the enemies of Jesus.

The United States has continually tied religion to nationalism in an effort to bolster the patriotic support of its citizens. This was especially true in the Cold War era. Throughout the 1940s, '50s, and '60s, it was widely recognized that the Soviets sought to remove religion from society. The term "godless communist" became commonplace in America. Not only were communists the enemies of America, they were the enemies of God.

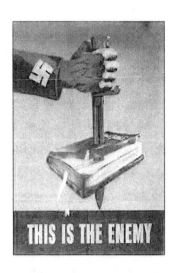

THIS IS THE ENEMY

The comic strip *This Godless Communism* was distributed to parochial schools from 1946–1972. It was designed to reveal the Soviet Union as materialistic and anti-religious in contrast to America's spiritual and idealistic character.

In a speech about communism in 1950, Senator Joseph McCarthy said, "Today we are engaged in a final, all-out battle between communistic atheism and Christianity."

In comic books, pamphlets, political speeches, and television shows, a concerted effort was made to characterize the Soviet Union as anti-God while America acknowledged the Almighty. It is noteworthy that "under God" was added to the Pledge of Allegiance in 1954 and "In God We Trust" was added to US currency ten years later (at the height of the Cold War).

For most of the 20th century, the connection between God, morality, and patriotism was reinforced constantly. The idea that godliness is next to "Americanness" became ingrained in American culture. Public displays of religion became essential to the American way of life. For many Americans, being a good patriot meant being a good Christian and vice versa. Any movement away from the public embrace of religion was a move toward societal degradation.

Even though many Americans accept the religious pluralism and cultural diversity that define our nation today, the root of nationalistic religion, which was planted in the middle of the last century, is still nestled in the heart of our national identity. These ideas shaped generations of Americans, and unless we approach the subject of nationalism and religion with humility and honesty, we will continue to see any changes to the American religious experience as an attack on our Christian way of life.

Modern Roots

By the 1980s, those who identified as Evangelical or Fundamentalist had become a powerful force that was shaping American politics. Opposition to abortion was the foundational issue of this newly formed Religious Right, but they also claimed support of Israel, opposition to feminism, opposition to environmental regulation, a foreign policy based on military strength, harsh punishment for criminals, conservative fiscal policy, and the elimination of entitlement programs. All of these positions had a basis in Fundamentalist theology.

Whenever a group of people insists on a particular perspective or lifestyle, they will face the opposition of those who disagree. Since the positions of the Religious Right are based largely on religious conviction, it is very easy for them to see political opposition as religious persecution.

Since the 1980s, the power of the Religious Right has waned, but its values have spread, giving it a broader influence than ever before. Ideas that were once espoused primarily by organizations like the Moral Majority are now broadcast by cable news and talk radio, proclaimed by politicians from Alaska to Louisiana, and promoted by numerous family values organizations.

In recent years the debate has become more aggressive and polarizing, giving birth to the greatest promoter of the persecution narrative— the Culture War.

The Culture of Persecution

For me, 2006 was an important year in the culture war. Conservative radio talk shows were at the height of their popularity. Fox News and MSNBC were proving that Americans enjoyed antagonistic bias from their news sources. Bill O'Reilly had just released his book *Culture Warrior*, and Christmas had become the ultimate battleground in the war between traditionalists and progressives.

At the time, I was a youth pastor, inspired primarily by Ron Luce and Teen Mania. Luce was a charismatic leader and was doing amazing things to motivate teens to aggressively take on the culture around them. The youth ministry that I led was thriving. We asked our teenagers to go beyond merely trying to fit in and to confront the culture and change it. We sought to eliminate the sale of pornography in our small town, and we wrote letters to companies that refused to acknowledge Christmas. We told our students that they could change the world.

Years later, one of those students, who is now an adult, told me about his struggles with Christianity. He told me about how, as a young person, he had wholeheartedly embraced the idea that if he did certain things, he could change the world. But the world didn't change. He had committed his youth to fighting the culture war, and it had failed. Now he was hesitant to give his time and energy to a faith that continued to make similar promises on which it would surely not deliver.

In ministry, as in politics, the culture war has been a convenient tool to inspire and motivate. It gave us purpose. It brought in money. It excited and motivated young people. But it was not real.

Fictitious Conflict

Private Teruo Nakamura was a Japanese soldier stationed on Morotai Island in Indonesia during World War II. The Allies captured the island of Morotai in 1944, but Nakamura hid in the jungle with other holdouts—until 1956. At that point Nakamura separated from his companions and built his own small fortress on the island. He defended his lonely outpost for eighteen years. He was discovered and arrested by the Indonesian air force on December 18, 1974. He was fifty-five years old.

During those 30 years of hiding out on Morotai, Teruo Nakamura most certainly heard rumors that the war had ended. He most certainly heard that the Allies had prevailed, Japan had surrendered, and the world was moving on. But Private Nakamura refused to believe it. He was committed to the war. The war was where he was most comfortable.

Nakamura died in a hospital in Taiwan four years after leaving his island. Sadly, Teruo Nakamura spent nearly thirty years, the majority of his life, engaged in a war that did not even exist.

In the same way, for the majority of Americans, the culture war does not really exist. It is an artificial conflict that political and religious zealots exploit in order to gain power and wealth.

Most Americans do not care if their cashier says "Merry Christmas" or "Happy Holidays." Most people just want an enjoyable holiday season. They don't want Christmas to be a battleground. Most Americans do not want to offend their neighbors, and if practicing their religion a bit less publicly will keep everyone happy, that is exactly what they will do. Most people have never experienced religious prejudice or been told they are not allowed to pray or express their faith in public. Most people are concerned about careers, homework, mowing the grass, doing the laundry, getting dinner on the table, and maybe enjoying some TV or a board game in the evening. The culture war does not figure into their daily concerns.

For most people, the battle for morality is also unnecessary. If there ever has been a culture war, we have already won. Our society values human life more than any society in history. We place extremely high importance on family and the involvement of parents in the lives of their children.

We care for the needy and the helpless. We value moral character, generosity, humility, kindness, and gratitude. We create stories where good guys win and bad guys lose. Our society certainly has many problems and many things to learn, but for the average American, life is pretty good.

The culture war is not a part of life in America unless we make it so. If political ideologues can convince us that all of society is embroiled in an epic struggle, then they win. Believing in the culture war is what makes it real.

At the same time, the notion of a culture war has an undeniable appeal. Everyone wants to be a hero, a brave crusader in the battle for truth, justice, and the American way. For many Americans, the idea of fighting for what is right is deeply ingrained into American history and culture. So, like Nakamura, we choose to soldier on, the last holdouts in a war that does not exist.

Who Benefits from Persecution?

Who benefits from the idea that we are engaged in a war for the soul of America? Those who are in the business of buying and selling power.

The culture war sells books, increases television viewership, and swells voter turnout. When politicians claim we are being oppressed, and they rally us to a cause, the nation does not benefit. The politicians benefit. More political contributions are made, and more people show up to vote, but the nation becomes more polarized, more divided, as a result.

Over the past decade or so, numerous commentators have used the persecution narrative as a central theme to sell books. Bill O'Reilly, Glenn Beck, Rush Limbaugh, Sarah Palin, Ann Coulter, and Todd Starnes are just some examples. Nearly every one of their books landed on the *New York Times* bestseller list. Clearly, the persecution narrative is quite profitable.

In 2014, Dinesh D'Souza released a book titled *America: Imagine a World without Her*, followed by a film of the same name. *America* highlights the greatness of the United States, downplays its flaws, and warns readers of the Obama Administration's policies that will destroy the country. While it is not specifically religious, the book and film fit neatly into the persecution narrative.

In July 2014, an uproar began when Costco removed *America* from its shelves. Accusations of anti-conservative bias and persecution swirled. At the same time Google was being accused of a similar bias because the word *America* did not automatically result in local movie theater schedules, as did searches for most other film titles. Both Google and Costco insisted there was no political motivation on their part. Costco claimed its decision was based upon sales, and Google claimed the word *America* was so generic that it did not trigger a movie theater search. Neither company wanted to be the center of a controversy, so *America* the film was placed at the top of Google's search results, and the book was returned to Costco's shelves.

The result of D'Souza's claim of persecution and this artificial controversy was that *America* the book became a bestseller, and *America* the film became a minor box office success.

As a troubling finale to this story, in September of 2014 D'Souza was convicted of breaking campaign finance laws by illegally contributing to a Senate candidate in New York. Despite this conviction, D'Souza has continued to insist that he has been unfairly targeted by the Obama administration. The judge who heard his case called such claims "nonsense" and said they were nothing but an effort to "deflect and minimize" the seriousness of D'Souza's crime.[7]

Who benefits from persecution? Candidates who want more votes, politicians who want more power, commentators who want more viewers, authors who want more book sales, and preachers who want more media coverage, bigger churches, and richer coffers. The idea that we are persecuted, whether for religious beliefs or any other ideology, is a myth perpetuated by the powerful. We should be suspicious whenever those in power claim persecution or try to rally the "persecuted." We should be especially suspicious if those in power claim to have the solution to this persecution, a solution from which they derive monetary or political gain.

> Even today a crude sort of persecution is all that is required to create an honourable name for any sect, no matter how indifferent in itself.
>
> —Friedrich Nietzche

While it should be clear by now why those in power find the persecution narrative so appealing, the following four chapters address the four specific "benefits" or results of the persecution narrative that make it so attractive to the masses.

3

Fear of Change

Like all humans, Christians value stability. Changing culture feels terribly unstable. As the values of the world shift, it can begin to feel that Christianity is being attacked.

Christianity's Position of Power

For about the past 1,500 years, Western culture has been dominated by Christianity. European and then American cultures were shaped by Christian history and values. Of course, Christianity changed significantly over these centuries: first influenced by the Roman Empire, then entered the Dark Ages, emerged as the most significant cultural and political power during the Renaissance, experienced schism and violence throughout the Reformation, and then combined with various developing philosophies during the Enlightenment.

Throughout the modern era, Western nations became the most powerful forces on the globe, influencing all corners of the earth through imperialism, trade, war, immigration, and media.

As Western Europe exported its culture throughout the world, it brought its form of Christianity to Africa, Asia, India, the Middle East, and the Americas.

While the formation of the United States was built upon unique religious principles—religious liberty, the lack of state-sponsored religion, the separation of church and state—it was still built upon ideals that emerged from a culture dominated by Christianity. This Christian-dominated culture continued in America for nearly two centuries.

Human beings have always had a difficult time separating religion from national identity or culture. For hundreds of years, spreading the Christian gospel was tied directly to exporting a Western way of life. Missionaries from Europe and America taught not only the message of Jesus but also a particular way of dressing, eating, speaking, and even having sex.

Even though the United States has no national religion or state-sponsored church, Christianity is still embedded deep within its foundations. Some people would like to identify the United States as a Christian nation, but religious liberty does not allow us to do so. The United States is a secular nation. This does not mean anti-religious. It simply means a-religious.

Even though the United States should never prefer a particular religious group, we must acknowledge that Christianity has been foundational to the formation, the values, and the culture of this country.

As a result, since the founding of this nation, Christians have enjoyed a position of privilege. We have expected our leaders to attend church and profess a desire to uphold Christian values. We expect Christianity to be understood and respected by our neighbors. We expect Christian religious leaders to hold positions of respect in society. We expect to get time off from work for Christian holidays.

For most of our history, people of other religions have been viewed with suspicion, if not animosity. We have churches on nearly every street corner, but places of worship for other religions are few and far between. Acknowledgment of the Christian God is on our money, in our Pledge of Allegiance, in our courtrooms, and at the start of public gatherings in many communities.

Only a few years ago Evangelicals were shaping the political, moral, and social landscape. This emergence of Evangelical Christians as a cultural influence came partly as a reaction to Roe v. Wade in 1973 and the cultural revolution of the 1960s and '70s. This emergence was also manipulated by people who wanted to form Christians into a voting bloc loyal to the Republican Party. For many Americans, the conservative political, social, and economic agenda became a part of their religious ethic.

From the late 1970s until around the turn of the millennium, conservative, Evangelical Christianity enjoyed a position of cultural power and became the dominant public face of Western Christianity. When many Americans hear the word *Christian*, they think of Focus on the Family, Jerry Falwell, *Left Behind*, and *Duck Dynasty*. Even though there are tens of millions of Christians around the world whose beliefs and practices are quite different, the Religious Right has defined Christianity in America.

Those who profess a fear of anti-Christian persecution in America are not just afraid that cultural forces are turning against them. They are afraid of losing their place of privilege in American society. A cultural shift is taking place around us, and many of us feel lost.

Losing My Religion

Because American culture is so closely tied to Christianity, cultural shifts can feel like attacks on religion. For years American society has followed a particular script that influenced every area of our lives:

history, the role of America globally, national policy, family values, gender roles, career paths, personal morality, and the function of religion. We have been a society which believes that a person's success or failure in life is based on his or her own discipline and determination. We have valued individuality, personal responsibility, and exceptionalism. Our culture has idealized the nuclear family where Dad works a job to pay the bills while Mom attends to domestic responsibilities, such as caring for children and cooking. We have valued a government that acknowledges God, does not restrict our liberties, and keeps everything in its place (including poor people and criminals). We have been a society run by white people, with a little smattering of color for variety.

In the 1960s, we experienced significant shifts in gender roles, personal morality, family structure, and racial boundaries. The cultural shifts have continued. Now we are seeing changes in the religious makeup, racial composition, and national origins of American society. Some anthropologists predict that Caucasians will be the minority in America by the year 2030.

In Todd Starnes's book *God Less America*, he alternates between stories of Christian persecution and sentimental memories of the good ol' days.

> Does the Christian persecution complex have an expiration date? Because ... uh ... you've all been in charge pretty much since ... uh ... what was that guy's name? ... Constantine. He converted in—what was it?—312 AD. I'm just saying, enjoy your success.
>
> —Jon Stewart, Comedy Central's *The Daily Show*

I grew up in a much simpler time," he says, "when blackberry was a pie and dirty dancing meant somebody forgot to clean out the barn for the square dance. It was a time when father still knew best—when girls were girls and men were men. I grew up in a time when a rainbow was a sign of God's promise, not gay rights.

This is the kind of refrain we often hear from those who fear the decay of traditional values. Starnes reminds us of days gone by with the hope that we will equate cultural change with moral deterioration. In many cases, that is exactly what we do. We see the world shifting, the reliable touchstones moving, and the face of America changing. It feels unknown and unstable, so we long for the comfortable world of the past.

It is not just the uncertainty of a changing culture that is disorienting. It is the fact that Christianity is quickly losing its position of cultural influence. We are no longer the ones in charge, and we don't know what to do about it. We no longer have the ear of the President. Legislation is no longer being shaped by Christian culture. We are becoming the marginalized minority, and the only way we know how to react is to cry "persecution."

Religious Pluralism

According to the Pew Research Center, 78 percent of Americans self-identified as Christians in 2007. Only a few years later, a 2012 study revealed that the number of Americans who identified as Christians had shrunk to 73 percent. Pew Research also found that during this period the religiously unaffiliated rose from 15 percent to just under 20 percent.[8]

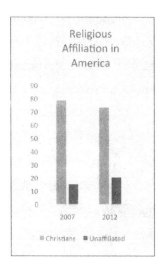

Even though a vast majority of Americans still identify as Christian, that number is shrinking, and the percentage of people who identify with other religions, or with no religion at all, is on the rise. In fact, the fastest growing religious affiliation in America is "none," and most of the "nones" are coming from the ranks of conservative Evangelicals.

At one time, the number of Americans who identified as Jewish, Muslim, or Hindu was negligible. Americans assumed that nearly every person they met on the street, at the supermarket, in school, or jogging through their neighborhood would identify with Christianity. This is no longer the case. We are still more likely to come in contact with Christians, but all of us know atheists, Jews, or Buddhists who work with us or live in our communities. As understanding of various religious traditions grows, more and more Americans feel the need to give consideration to people of faiths other than Christianity.

It is easy for Christians to see some of this consideration as an assault on Christian tradition. When retail stores choose not to highlight Christmas, it may feel that they are attempting to exclude Christians. This is not the case. These businesses are simply attempting to consider their customers who might feel excluded by our culture's focus on the Christian celebration.

Thinking about the way others may be excluded by our traditions is not compromising our convictions or religious identity. Considering others is caring and loving, which is the essence of Christianity.

Science and Religion

Since the time of Copernicus and the beginning of the Enlightenment, science and religion have had a tenuous relationship. Copernicus's assertion that the earth rotated around the sun, rather than the reverse, came into conflict with the Church's teaching (based on their understanding of Scripture) that the earth was the immovable center of the universe. Prior to the Enlightenment, religion and science (also called natural philosophy) had functioned in the same arena and, for the most part, supported each other. From the fourteenth century until today, science has been seen progressively as a pursuit that is separate from religion. Many people now believe science and religion are not only separate pursuits but in conflict with each other.

The New Atheism movement, emerging at the start of the 21st century, has sought to marginalize religious belief as the enemy of science and reason. Richard Dawkins, who has been identified as one of the Four Horsemen of New Atheism (along with the late Christopher Hitchens, Sam Harris, and Daniel Dennett), has made this statement more than once: "When two opposite points of view are expressed with equal intensity, the truth does not necessarily lie exactly halfway between them. It is possible for one side to be simply wrong." Dawkins is attempting to point out that an argument for evolution is not equal to an argument for creationism or the existence of God. I believe that Dawkins is overly antagonistic and is unfairly biased against Christianity, but I also believe there is an important point at the heart of his comment above. Christians have often been too slow to admit that they might be wrong.

Militant atheists have tried to position science as the enemy of religion. This is a problematic strategy, but one that Christians have also attempted to utilize. It is a mistake to assert that Christianity is the enemy of certain scientific perspectives or ideas. Doing so puts us in a position where we cannot admit we are wrong. If our position is tied to the opposition of another position, any admission of fault is ceding ground to the enemy. In a struggle for cultural superiority, one cannot ever give up ground. This can cause Christians to become entrenched in outdated and disproven ideas simply because they cannot admit they are wrong.

Throughout history, whenever the Church has taken a stand against a particular scientific theory, eventually, it has had to admit its mistake and adjust its doctrine. Scripture has been used to defend all sorts of faulty ideas, including a geocentric universe, slavery, imperialism, genocide, and racism. Some Christians have declared in vitro fertilization or heart transplants to be immoral and against the will of God. As the Church has come to understand its mistakes, it has had to adjust its interpretation of certain Scriptures. We now recognize that Psalm 93:1, "He has established the world; it shall never be moved," is not a scientific description regarding the design of the universe, as medieval Christians assumed. We need to approach science with humility, knowing that our understanding of God and Scripture may be faulty and in need of future adjustment.

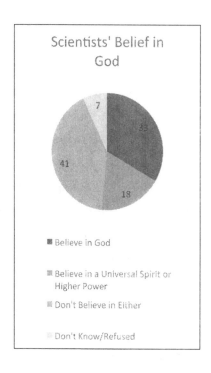

While there are certainly scientists who believe that religious conviction is at odds with scientific progress, this group is a minority. A Pew Research study found that 51 percent of scientists who are members of the American Association for the Advancement of Science believe in God, a universal spirit, or a higher power.[9] The idea that a majority of scientists are atheist or want to disprove the existence of God is simply not true.

Scientists are not activists. We are sometimes led to believe that scientific research has a particular agenda. Agenda-driven science, though, is bad science. Good scientists go where the evidence leads. If a researcher is attempting to prove a particular perspective or support a particular agenda, the result will be faulty. The same goes for the religious person who wants to use science to support his or her belief. The result will be flawed. This is bad science.

To believe that science in general or scientists in particular are trying to persecute Christians is to accuse the scientific community of bad, agenda-driven science. Scientific discovery and research in recent years have brought us tremendous amounts of knowledge about the universe, and it has brought us amazingly useful products. New understanding of the tiniest particles is giving us a shocking understanding of the universe. Medical research is allowing us to treat diseases that were once considered incurable. Energy research is revealing ways we can power our homes, transportation, and industries without continuing to damage our environment.

We can allow these discoveries to point us toward a naturalistic and mechanical perspective of the universe, or we can allow these discoveries to inspire greater awe of the Creator. Science can bring us new understanding of God. A growing understanding of the wonders of the universe can cause us to worship God more, not question God's existence. Science should be an ally of Christianity, not its enemy.

Gay Rights

For years we have been warned about the "gay agenda." Homosexuals have been accused of horrible behavior and a desire to open the floodgates of immorality on society. As time has gone on, many of us have realized that the only agenda held by most gay people is the desire for acceptance and respect.

However, not everyone has come to believe this, and some are still attempting to demonize gay people. On July 23, 2014, Congresswoman Michele Bachmann appeared on the conservative radio show *Faith & Liberty*. She talked about the gay community's agenda to force their lifestyle on all Americans.

> This is their ultimate goal, to not allow for diversity of opinion on this issue. They don't want to be celebrated, but they want to force everyone to not only agree with them, but to finance their agenda." Bachmann went on to accuse gay people of wanting to legalize polygamy and child rape. "I think also, they want to abolish age of consent laws, which means we would do away with statutory rape laws, so that adults would be able to freely prey on little children sexually.[10]

That is certainly an example of a politician attempting to instill fear in her constituency to incite them to action. It is like saying, "If you vote for my opponents, they will let people rape your children." It is also an attempt to characterize a group of people as a significant threat to Christian values. This is scapegoating: pinning the guilt for societal ills on one person or group of people.

Politicians and preachers have been guilty of scapegoating as long as there have been politicians and preachers. They have also been guilty of scapegoating the gay community for decades, telling the American people, without any evidence, that homosexuals are predisposed to rape, incest, pedophilia, sexual promiscuity, and every kind of sexual deviance, and that homosexuals want to impose their immorality on all of society.

Many Christians have learned to fear persecution from the gay community. In reality, the gay community has endured far more abuse than it has inflicted. I have a friend who recently spoke to Dan Haseltine, lead singer of the Christian band Jars of Clay, regarding a Twitter conversation on the topic of gay marriage. Dan tweeted some questions regarding gay marriage in an attempt to stir some honest conversation. Some thoughtful and some terribly negative responses flooded in for several days. Dan said to my friend, "If we have treated gay people as badly as I was treated, we have a lot to apologize for."

I know a man who has gone to Pride parades for several years with his family. They hold signs that read, "I am a Christian, and I am sorry for the way that my religion has treated you." Every time, he and his family receive hugs, tears, and "I-forgive-yous." This is a beautiful expression of Jesus' love rather than accusations and condemnation.

It is important for us to be aware of the pain Christianity has caused in its stand for "biblical truth." According to the Centers for Disease Control, gay teens are four times more likely than straight teens to commit suicide.[11] A recent study by the American Association of Suicidology seems to indicate that homosexual teens who received counseling from religious leaders were more likely to attempt suicide than those who did not seek help.[12] This is incredibly troubling, and it should cause us to consider the way we communicate our beliefs.

Christianity's relationship with homosexuals displays one of the greatest dangers of the persecution complex. The claim of victimhood invariably turns us into victimizers. When we imagine that we are the persecuted, we inevitably become the persecutor.

Instead of fear that gay people are attempting to impose immorality on us all, the world could benefit a great deal from our demonstration of love, compassion, and humility. The conflict over the issue of homosexuality gives us the opportunity to ask for forgiveness, to provide care and compassion to people who have been abused and marginalized, and to welcome those who may be different from us.

30+ Examples of Christian Privilage
By Sam Killerman

1. You can expect to have time off work to celebrate religious holidays.

2. Music and television programs pertaining to your religion's holidays are readily accessible.

3. It is easy to find stores that carry items that enable you to practice your faith and celebrate religious holidays.

4. You aren't pressured to celebrate holidays from another faith that may conflict with your religious values.

5. Holidays celebrating your faith are so widely supported you can often forget they are limited to your faith (e.g. wish someone a "Merry Christmas" or "Happy Easter" without considering their faith).

6. You can worship freely, without fear of violence or threats.

7. A bumper sticker supporting your religion won't likely lead to your car being vandalized.

8. You can practice your religious customs without being questioned, mocked, or inhibited.

9. If you are being tried in court, you can assume that the jury of "your peers" will share your faith and not hold that against you in weighing decisions.

10. When swearing an oath, you will place your hand on a religious scripture pertaining to your faith.

11. Positive references to your faith are seen dozens a time a day by everyone, regardless of their faith.

12. Politicians responsible for your governance are probably members of your faith.

13. Politicians can make decisions citing your faith without being labeled as heretics or extremists.

14. It is easy for you to find your faith accurately depicted in television, movies, books, and other media.

15. You can reasonably assume that anyone you encounter will have a decent understanding of your beliefs.

16. You will not be penalized (socially or otherwise) for not knowing other people's religious customs.

17. Your faith is accepted/supported at your workplace.

18. You can go into any career you want without it being associated with or explained by your faith.

19. You can travel to any part of the country and know your religion will be accepted, safe, and you will have access to religious spaces to practice your faith.

20. Your faith can be an aspect of your identity without being a defining aspect (e.g., people won't think of you as their "Christian" friend)

21. You can be polite, gentle, or peaceful, and not be considered an "exception" to those practicing your faith.

22. Fundraising to support congregations of your faith will not be investigated as potentially threatening or terrorist behavior.

23. Construction of spaces of worship will not likely be halted due to your faith.

24. You are never asked to speak on behalf of all the members of your faith.

25. It is unlikely you will be judged by the actions of other members of your faith.

26. You can go anywhere and assume you will be surrounded by members of your faith.

27. Without special effort, your children will have a multitude of teachers who share your faith.

28. Without special effort, your children will have a multitude of friends who share your faith.

29. It is easily accessible for you or your children to be educated from kindergarten through post-grad at institutions of your faith.

30. Disclosing your faith to an adoption agency will not likely prevent you from being able to adopt children.

31. In the event of a divorce, the judge won't immediately grant custody of your children to your ex because of your faith.

32. Your faith is taught or offered as a course at most public institutions.

33. You can complain about your religion being under attack without it being perceived as an attack on another religion.

34. You can dismiss the idea that identifying with your faith bears certain privileges.

Everyday Feminism. November 11, 2012. http://everydayfeminism.com/2012/11/30-examples-of-christian-privilege/

4

Addiction to Certainty

Recently this post came across my Facebook newsfeed:

> Before You go out today, If You can Type
> "Amen|" In 2Secs. From Your Mobile Device
> or computer. Your Destiny Helper Shall Locate
> You Before Today Ends and idea to become
> great will come you in Jesus name. If You
> believe & is Sure You Have A Destiny. Type
> Amen. Am 100% sure so don't Ignore.

This post said it was from well-known pastor T. D. Jakes, but it actually came from a page that isn't affiliated with him. Nevertheless, it was liked by nearly 5,000 people and shared over 400 times.

I decided to interact with some fans at this T. D. Jakes page. It has thousands of followers who respond to, like, and share the page's manipulative posts every single day. When I tried explaining that this was a fake page and certainly did not represent the real Bishop Jakes, many of them became incredibly defensive. Even when I gave a link to the real, verified T. D. Jakes page, they refused to believe.

Knowing for certain has been a value of American Evangelicalism. We have clung tightly to our ideas with pride and confidence despite glaring evidence to the contrary. In fact, it seems that we cling even more tightly when we face opposition to those beliefs. This is a problem.

Becoming More Entrenched

In recent years, alcohol consumption has become less of an issue for Evangelicals than it once was. Where many American churches once condemned the consumption of alcohol, they now accept that having a drink can be a valuable part of culture that is not condemned by Scripture.

A Lutheran church in Denver Colorado holds an annual event called the "Blessing of the Bicycles." Hundreds of residents of the community join the church for a bike ride, prayer, fellowship, and a keg of Fat Tire ale (which uses a picture of a bicycle for its logo). This event has broken down barriers and given the church an opportunity to connect with all kinds of Denver residents.

"Beer and Hymns" events have even become regular occurrences in churches across the country. Church members gather at the church or at a local pub to enjoy beer and old-fashioned hymns. This loosening of restrictions has concerned the Southern Baptist Convention. Rather than consider adjusting their rigid, prohibition-era position on alcohol, the Southern Baptist Convention entrenched on the issue with a new resolution in 2006, reasserting their objection to even moderate alcohol consumption, sales, or manufacturing.[13]

When the world changes, we become very uncomfortable. Our response is to dig in, to entrench. As Christians, we are often committed to tradition and to traditional values. When the world changes, it can feel like the world is moving away from us—or maybe even against us. It is natural to cling to what we know and try to hold the world back. It is natural for us to desire what is familiar and relatable while resisting change.

Fundamentalism and Certainty

In his book *The War of Art*, Steven Pressfield says,

> Fundamentalism is the philosophy of the powerless, the conquered, the displaced and the dispossessed. Its spawning ground is the wreckage of political and military defeat, as Hebrew fundamentalism arose during Babylonian captivity, as white Christian fundamentalism appeared in the American South during Reconstruction, as the notion of

the Master Race arose in Germany following World War I. In such desperate times, the vanquished race would perish without a doctrine that restored hope and pride. Islamic fundamentalism ascended from the same landscape of despair and possesses the same tremendous and potent appeal.

Pressfield asserts that any kind of fundamentalism is the enemy of creativity and art.

> Fundamentalists (or more accurately, the beleaguered individual who embraces fundamentalism) cannot stand freedom. He cannot find his way into the future, so he retreats to the past. He returns in imagination to the glory days of his race and seeks to reconstitute both them and himself in their purer, more virtuous light. He gets back to basics. To fundamentals.[14]

Christians who long for the past are those who are most likely to embrace the persecution narrative. These are Christians who are pessimistic about the future of society. They believe the best is behind us: the Garden of Eden, the days of Jesus, the early Church, the time of America's founding, or the 1950s. They often speak of getting back to the values and morality of the past. They talk about how a man's word used to be his bond and how children used to respect adults.

Fundamentalism also says, "I know best." In the preface to *On Being Certain*, author Dr. Robert Burton, a neurologist, says,

> Certainty is everywhere. Fundamentalism is in full bloom. Legions of authorities cloaked in total conviction tell us why we should invade country X, ban *The Adventures of Huckleberry Finn* in schools, or eat stewed tomatoes; how much brain damage is necessary to justify a plea of diminished capacity; the precise moment when a sperm and an egg must be treated as a human being; and why the stock market will eventually revert to historical returns. A public change of mind is national news.[15]

While Burton goes on to explore the scientific aspects of certainty, the opening of his book identify a deep problem: believing that we know something for certain nearly always leads to dysfunction.

When we claim persecution, it is often with an air of fundamentalism. The idea of persecution confirms our rightness, and we become all the more rigid in our beliefs. Belief in Christian persecution is, just as Pressfield asserts, a desire for what is behind and a fear of the unknown that lies ahead.

Need for the Familiar

Human beings have a need for the familiar. Dr. Burton also examines the brain science behind the idea of knowing in his book *On Being Certain*. His work reveals that our brains experience a reward when we encounter the expected. This pushes us toward experiences that are familiar. Burton proposes that this reward is very similar to the neurological reward associated with addiction.

> Research into addictions to drugs, alcohol, gambling, and cigarettes has been instrumental in revealing how behavior is rewarded. The general principle equally applicable to the worst cocaine addiction, stamp collecting, or idle musings is that for a behavior to persist, there must be some brain-mediated reward.[16]

Burton asserts that the chemical reward experienced in the brain of the prolific stamp collector upon acquiring a stamp missing from his or her collection, the gambler whose number comes up, or the video gamer who aligns a row of matching jewels is quite similar to the drug addict getting high from cocaine. These experiences release dopamine in the brain that gives us pleasure at encountering the predictable. Certainty, encountering the predictable over and over again is addictive. "Might the know-it-all personality trait be seen as an addiction to the feeling of knowing?" asks Dr. Burton.

A 2009 *Psychology Today* article titled "A Hunger for Certainty" asserts exactly the same idea. "Like an addiction to anything, when the craving for certainty is met there is a sensation of reward."[17]

Fundamentalism is an addiction to familiarity. Addiction to familiarity is an addiction to certainty.

We are accustomed to Christian dominance. We are comfortable with a culture where pervasive Christianity is taken for granted. We know what to expect from such a society. We know the rules. We know each person's place. This kind of environment gives us a rewarding sense of knowing. It gives us certainty.

The problem is that the world is changing, and our sense of certainty is slipping away. This sense of certainty is completely entangled with our ideas about Christian faith, therefore it is natural to see a disruption of our certainty as an attack on our faith.

5

The Narrative Perpetuates Itself

Many of us remember the (supposed) road-rage epidemic of the mid-nineties. Local and national news sources made us acutely aware of the angry and aggressive drivers who purportedly shared the roadways with us. The National Highway Transportation Safety Administration declared that two-thirds of highway deaths, 28,000 per year, could be attributed to aggressive driving.[18] Daniel Gardner, in his book *The Science of Fear*, discusses the road rage obsession and shows how sensationalism in the media leads to a distorted view of reality, just as it did in the "Summer of the shark."

> If the road-rage panic were to be subjected to examination, it might reasonably be suggested that its rise and fall simply reflected the reality on American roads. But the evidence doesn't support such an assertion. "Headlines notwithstanding, there was not—there is not—the least statistical or other scientific evidence of more aggressive driving on our nation's

roads," concluded journalist Michael Fumento in a detailed examination of the alleged epidemic published in *The Atlantic Monthly* in August 1998.

Gardner goes on to explain the process that creates incidents like the road-rage craze.

> More reporting puts more examples and more emotions into more brains. Public concern rises, and reporters respond with more reporting. More reporting, more fear; more fear, more reporting. The feedback loop is established and fear steadily grows.[19]

In the same way, media sources, politicians, and preachers who report anti-Christian persecution are creating the same type of feedback loop. Many conservative politicians, authors, and talk show hosts are feeding American Evangelicals a continual diet of persecution complex hype. As American Evangelicals absorb this hype, concern rises, and preachers and pundits respond with more reports of persecution. More reporting, more fear; more fear, more reporting.

Christian Persecution in Music

"Jesus Freak" was the Christian rock song that identified a generation of young Christians. The band DC Talk released it in 1995. The nineties was the era of

Suppose one reads a story of filthy atrocities in the paper. Then suppose that something turns up suggesting that the story might not be quite true, or not quite so bad as it was made out. Is one's first feeling, `Thank God, even they aren't quite so bad as that,' or is it a feeling of disappointment, and even a determination to cling to the first story for the sheer pleasure of thinking your enemies as bad as possible? If it is the second then it is, I am afraid, the first step in a process which, if followed to the end, will make us into devils

70

contemporary Christian music, and DC Talk ruled this decade. The chorus of "Jesus Freak" goes like this:

What will people think
When they hear that I'm a Jesus freak
What will people do when they find that it's true
I don't really care if they label me a Jesus freak
There ain't no disguising the truth

DC Talk went on to release two books, *Jesus Freaks* and *Jesus Freaks: Volume 2*, which told the stories of historic martyrs and people who suffered because of their Christian faith. DC Talk had a tremendous influence on a generation of Christian young people. *Jesus Freak* helped to cement in the minds of Christian teens of the nineties that Christianity is under attack.

Christian Persecution in Film

Evangelicals have been producing films with explicit Christian messages since the 1970s. As filmmaking has become a more affordable endeavor, the frequency, sophistication, and variety of these faith-oriented films has increased. Whether the quality of these films has improved is debatable.

As with the major Hollywood studios, the movies produced for a Christian audience seem to go through

You see, one is beginning to wish that black was a little blacker. If we give that wish its head, later on we shall wish to see grey as black, and then to see white itself as black. Finally, we shall insist on seeing everything - God and our friends and ourselves included - as bad, and not be able to stop doing it: we shall be fixed for ever in a universe of pure hatred.

—C. S. Lewis, from *Mere Christianity*

phases. For a while we saw a lot of films dealing with the Antichrist and the end times. Then we saw a spate of films centered on family relationships. In recent years, the theme of anti-Christian persecution has taken on prominence. *God's Not Dead* is far from the only the film that feed the persecution complex, as discussed earlier in the book, it is merely one of the most recent and most successful.

A lesser known but more egregious film was released in July 2014. Called *Persecuted*, it is the story of John Luther, certainly a reference to Martin Luther, who stood against the religious corruption of his day. In the film, Luther is America's most well-known and respected Christian evangelist. Luther is framed for murder after refusing to support legislation that would require religions in America to give equal time to all other religions. Presumably, this would mean that a Christian church would be forced to make time to hear from Buddhists, Muslims, and Scientologists. The film takes no time to explain why this would be bad legislation or why Luther's position is correct. *Persecuted* takes for granted that its audience will understand that pluralism is bad, legislation that prefers Christianity is good, and those who stand against the encroachment of other religions on American life are heroes.

Persecuted is designed to instill fear in its audience; fear that the United States government is not far from persecuting Christians in the name of tolerance, religious pluralism, and national security. *New York Times* film critic Neil Genzlinger wrote,

> This terrible attempt at a political thriller for the religious right is aimed not at Christians in general but at a certain breed of them, the kind who feel as if the rest of the world were engaged in a giant conspiracy against their interpretation of good and truth.

The film subtly equates traditional conservativism with Christian values. *Persecuted* creates an exaggerated image of persecution to perpetuate the persecution narrative and stir Evangelicals to action. Genzlinger concludes his review by saying,

> What are those goals? No need to say, because all that this film, written and directed by Daniel Lusko, is really trying to do is push the "we are persecuted" button of its intended audience. In the movie, as in real life, that narrative needs no specifics about who is doing this persecuting or why or how.[20]

Stories of Fear

Stories are a powerful means of conveying a message—perhaps the most powerful. Both fiction and non-fiction stories strengthen ideas.

It does not matter if the story is made up or reported truth; our brains respond the same to both.[21] Stories of persecution condition our brains to expect more persecution. These stories train us to believe that anti-Christian persecution is a very real and widespread problem that should be feared by every Christian. Daniel Gardner addresses this in *The Science of Fear*.

> Storytelling may be natural. It may also be enlightening. But there are many ways in which it is a lousy tool for understanding the world we live in and what really threatens us. Anecdotes aren't data, as scientists say, no matter how moving they may be or how they pile up.[22]

Unfortunately, most information regarding anti-Christian persecution in America is anecdotal. Anecdotes are what we hear on Fox News when Todd Starnes talks about religious persecution, or on the Glenn Beck show when he talks about the culture war, or at church on Sunday morning when our preacher warns us about encroachments on our religious liberty. These stories are powerful. They stir our emotions and move us to action. But we should always be somewhat skeptical of anecdotes that are not attached to data.

PART 2

Why is the Persecution Narrative So Attractive

6

Persecution Creates Community

One of the most attractive qualities of persecution is its ability to create solidarity among the persecuted. This is one reason why so many minorities and subcultures claim to be the recipient of persecutory violence. Whether the persecution is real is irrelevant. Even imaginary persecution binds communities together.

Victimization and Community

When a group of people experiences discrimination or abuse, when they are victimized, their collective bond is strengthened. Members of a marginalized or victimized group often become more loyal to that group because of the persecution they experience (or imagine they experience). This is a powerful concept. Throughout history we have seen leaders take advantage of the ability of persecution to create strength, loyalty, and action within a community.

During the Middle Ages, the emergence of the Black Death was mysterious, gruesome, and deadly. Lacking any other viable explanation, people throughout Europe blamed the Jews for the emergence and spread of this plague. Rumors that Jews were poisoning water supplies spread quickly from one town to another. Many in Europe already believed Jews were plotting the destruction of Christianity and European society in general. In this anti-Semitic context, it was no great leap to believe that Jews were taking action against them. For communities throughout Europe in great need of hope, this persecution complex gave them something to rally behind: anti-Semitic violence. Thousands of Jewish people were killed as a result of the fear and paranoia surrounding the Black Death. Hundreds of Jewish communities in Europe were completely destroyed between the years 1348–1350.

As I noted earlier, even imaginary persecution creates community. For the suffering communities throughout Europe during the time of the Black Death, imagining that they were dying at the hands of Jews gave them something to fight, a reason to live. Their unified purpose became the destruction of Jews. This story also shows how easily the perception of persecution can turn the victims into victimizers, because at the root of the persecution narrative is the desire for self-preservation.

One of the defining issues of our time is sexual identity. We see both proponents and opponents of gay rights using the persecution card to bring stability and unity to their constituency. The conservative traditionalists claim to be under assault by LGBT supporters who want to tear down the foundations of decency and morality. Meanwhile, LGBT supporters claim to bear the prejudice and bigotry of religious fundamentalism. Both sides want to be the victim, because victimization creates community through claims that members of the persecuted group occupy the moral high ground.

The death of Matthew Shepard has become a rallying point for the cause of gay rights. He was a gay man who was attacked and killed in Laramie, Wyoming in October 1998. Two men picked up Shepard, drove him to a rural area, beat and robbed him, and left him for dead tied to a fence. Shepard was discovered eighteen hours later by a cyclist. He never recovered consciousness, dying in a hospital five days later.

Most people involved in the case concluded that Shepard was targeted because he was gay. Not everyone has accepted this account though. In 2013 (fifteen years after the incident), Stephen

Jimenez published *The Book of Matt: Hidden Truths about the Murder of Matthew Shepard,* which argued that Shepard was merely the victim of a drug deal gone wrong. The book has been widely panned as speculative and full of fictional accounts, and yet many people have latched onto this theory. Following the release of this book, conservative radio host Sandy Rios called Shepard's story "a complete fraud" while trying to paint the LGBT community as deviants who are bent on societal degradation.

For the LGBT community, Matthew Shepard is a symbol of the prejudice and violence that has been perpetrated against individuals because of their sexual orientation. They identify with his victimization, and this victimization helps to strengthen their resolve and legitimize their cause. On both sides of the coin, the suggestion of persecution creates community, whether or not the literal facts support each side's chosen narrative.

Those who oppose the advancement of gay rights recognize that Shepard's death strengthens the LGBT community. The conservative, traditionalist community cannot be the victim if Matthew Shepard is seen as an LGBT martyr. The solution is to delegitimize the persecution of Shepard. If he was simply a drug dealer, then his position as an LGBT martyr is destroyed, and conservatives can insert themselves into the position of the persecuted party. Just as persecution by traditionalists helps to strengthen the gay rights community, so persecution by gay rights activists helps to strengthen social conservatives. The one thing both sides have in common is their willingness to play fast and loose with the facts to their advantage.

Seeking to describe this phenomenon, writer Ta-Nehisi Coates made the following statement in *The Atlantic* in 2010:

> Racism tends to attract attention when it's flagrant and filled with invective. But like all bigotry, the most potent component of racism is frame-flipping—positioning the bigot as the actual victim. So the gay do not simply want to marry; they want to convert our children into sin. The Jews do not merely want to be left in peace; they actually are plotting world take-over. And the blacks are not actually victims of American power, but beneficiaries of the war against hard-working whites.[23]

Everyone wants to be the victim. Victimhood lends legitimacy to our cause. Victimhood creates community.

The Persecuted Becomes the Persecutor

In the same way that victimization creates unity amongst those who have suffered similar circumstances—war, kidnapping, natural disasters, or abuse—violence also has a strong unifying effect on those who perpetuate it. We see this when a community forms around the marginalization of a particular group: e.g. Muslims, homosexuals, immigrants, or ethnic minorities-. The oppressed group is nearly always identified as the source of a problem. Immigrants are blamed for the decline of available jobs. Homosexuals are blamed for moral decline. Following the Civil War, African-Americans were blamed for many financial and social difficulties. Today, blacks are often the scapegoats for the problems of crime and poverty.

In 2011, the Occupy Movement spread quickly across the United States and around the globe. While Occupy participants would claim disparate goals for their protests and activities, their real, unifying impetus was opposition to the rich. Occupy communities were bound together by their belief that the world's economic problems were caused by the ultra-rich 1 percent and the widening gap between rich and poor.

Most communities, groups, or movements are established because of their opposition to another group or activity. Abolitionists opposed the injustice of slavery. Communism opposed the greed and inequality of capitalism. The civil rights movement opposed the inequity of American culture toward African Americans. The Moral Majority opposed the moral decay of America. The climate change movement opposes environmental irresponsibility. The Tea Party opposes big government. The ice bucket challenge opposes the disease ALS. Of course, communism cannot fight against the abstract *ideas* of capitalism, greed, and inequality. Soviets found the embodiment of these abstractions in the United States. The Moral Majority could not do battle with immorality, so opposition was targeted at Democrats and the media. It has been said that a movement does not need a god, but every movement needs a devil. Even if these opposition groups do not carry out violent action, it can certainly be argued that their opposition is a form of pent-up violence. The purpose of the group is to defeat and destroy the other. This is violent intent.

The Bible points out the problem of violent intent several times. In 1 John 3:15, for instance, we read, "All who hate a brother or sister are murderers,

> "You have heard that it was said to those of ancient times, 'You shall not murder'; and 'whoever murders shall be liable to judgment.' But I say to you that if you are angry with a brother or sister, you will be liable to judgment; and if you insult a brother or sister, you will be liable to the council; and if you say, 'You fool,' you will be liable to the hell of fire."
>
> Matthew 5:21–22

and you know that murderers do not have eternal life abiding in them."

This unifying effect of violence is displayed especially well in the short story *The Lottery* by Shirley Jackson. This story describes how a small village in rural America chooses one person each year to kill. This ritual killing brings peace to the community—until the next year, when they do it all over again.

A more recent incarnation of this concept of ritual killing and unifying violence is seen in *The Hunger Games*. The destructive tendencies of the civilization are suppressed by the annual display of violence and sacrifice perpetrated against a few people.

The Purge film franchise also displays strong similarities to *The Lottery* and *The Hunger Games* by presenting a society whose peace is based on the annual tradition of the Purge: one night where citizens vent their pent-up violence on each other without repercussion.

All of these stories reveal the primal tendency of humanity to build a peaceful society upon the violence perpetuated against a few. When blame is heaped on an individual or group of people and they are punished, the rest of society is able to live in peace.[24]

Christian Leadership and Community

We hear the same old story at churches and political rallies throughout America. First, the speaker describes an account of violent persecution of Christians in another country or another time in history. Then he or she goes on to tell his listeners that Christians are being persecuted right here in America by the stripping away of religious liberty and by anti-religious or anti-Christian activism on issues like abortion, homosexuality, health care, gun rights, immigration, feminism, environmentalism, evolution, and immorality in the media. We recognize that our problems are not as bad as first-century Christians, who were literally fed to the lions, but as the speaker rails against the deterioration of Christian America, we become convinced that we have become an oppressed minority. The world is against us. We must band together. We must take action.

The Sunday morning preacher who works hard to convince his congregation of the persecution of American Christians is using the issue of persecution to create a stronger community.

85

Christians who believe the world is against them form stronger churches. They are generally more committed to their fellow believers. They attend more weekly church meetings. They are more involved in ministry. They give more money. They are more committed to evangelism and taking action against social evils.

The promotion of victimization is a powerful tool for religious or political leaders. As leaders, we should be careful not to exploit people by claiming persecution where none actually exists. As followers, we should be a bit suspicious of leaders who claim that we are the victims of persecution.

Culture Unites—And Divides

Any time a person brings up James Bond, the conversation inevitably evolves into a debate over who is the better Bond—Sean Connery, Timothy Dalton, Roger Moore, Pierce Brosnan, or Daniel Craig. If there are more than three people in this conversation, someone might even suggest the best Bond is George Lazenby (the often forgotten actor who played James Bond in only one film). We fight about who makes the best 007 not because we really have differing opinions but because we cannot help but divide. We divide over everything. Pepsi or Coke? Catholic or Protestant? Superman or Batman? King James or NIV? Paper or plastic? We have a built-in desire to disagree and divide into cliques, tribes, and denominations. It seems to be a part of human nature.

I have a nephew who insists that RC is the best cola, Aquaman is the greatest superhero, and Detroit is America's greatest city. We probably all know someone like him. It is not simply the desire to be contrary, it is the desire to be distinct that drives these minority opinions. We fear becoming an undifferentiated mass, because we know that will lead inevitably to conflict as we seek to create a pecking order. We are constantly engaged in differentiation in order to prevent such a struggle.

We all have the need for community and acceptance, but we also have the need to be distinct and separate. This is even truer for emerging generations than it was in the past.

Those who are Millennials and younger seem to have little need to identify with large groups. They are quite content to find their identity in smaller tribes. Young people are not joiners. In decades past, people identified themselves by the groups of which they were a part. They joined civic groups, denominations, and social clubs. All of these organizational structures are now declining, because young people do not have the need for affiliation with large groups. The fastest growing religious affiliation in America is "none," and the fastest growing political affiliation is independent.[25]

This has become a problem for many charitable organizations that rely on individual donations. I work with Habitat for Humanity, an organization that strives to make home ownership a reality for needy people. In the past, donors have been proud to support Habitat. The organization does good work and has a strong reputation. People made Habitat a regular part of their monthly or annual giving. They were pleased to identify themselves with the group.

Now fundraisers are finding that younger generations are not interested in supporting specific organizations like Habitat for Humanity. They do not feel fulfilled by identifying themselves with well-established, reliable, or respected organizations as did past generations. Millennials are interested in supporting the cause, not the organization.

Donate.ly founder Javan Van Gronigen spoke to *Time* magazine about this issue in 2012. "Before our generation, you saw my parents would be like, 'Oh, we want to give to the Red Cross,'" he said. "My generation would say we want to give to education or to fighting child slavery. Now it's going even deeper and the next generation is saying, 'I want to save that person right there."[26]

The tendency of younger people to diverge from the majority is built into all of us to some degree. This is why when the church decides to install red carpet, there will always be a contingent that wants blue carpet. When a school chooses to make its mascot the eagle, there will always be a group who prefers the wombat. When a business adds color to its logo, there will always be those who liked the black-and-white version better.

Culture divides. We see examples of this at the beginning of the Bible. Genesis tells us that after Cain killed his brother Abel, he went off to begin his own society. This is not simply a punishment, for God vowed to protect Cain. When humanity is consolidating its efforts at the Tower of Babel, God disperses them. These stories give us an original archetype for the continual dividing of societal groups.

When we say, "Society would be better if everyone followed the Bible," there will always be people who say, "No, the Bible is not a good model," or, "I don't agree with your interpretation of the Bible," or, "We should also be following the holy books of other religions."

When we say, "Public assemblies should open with prayer," someone will say, "I don't want to pray," or, "My religion has different types of prayer." This dissention is not persecution; it is a natural function of culture, which can serve to make our society better. When we consider diverse ideas, perspectives, and opinions, we become a richer, healthier, more caring, and more thoughtful society.

7

Persecution Rallies People to Action

In October 2013, the Values Voters Summit was held in Washington, DC. Conservative voters gathered to hear from Republican and Tea Party celebrities like Ted Cruz, Rand Paul, and Glenn Beck. The year 2013 seemed to be a high point in the recent polarization in American politics. The major parties were gathering supporters behind their positions on hot-button issues.

The primary purpose of the Values Voters Summit is to rally support for conservative candidates and stir voters to action. It has also become an important event for conservative presidential hopefuls. It is their opportunity to prove they are worthy of the conservative base's support.

The 2013 event featured a recurring theme: the persecution of American Christians. Senator Rand Paul spoke about a "worldwide war on Christianity" being ignored by President Obama. Ted Cruz talked about soldiers being forbidden from expressing their faith. Senator Rick Santorum talked about the forces of the left "trying to silence you, because their secular religion is okay, but yours is not." E. W. Jackson talked about "a growing hostility toward Christians," saying, "They want us to put the Bible aside. They want us to divorce ourselves from our faith."[27]

THINGS
EVANGELICALS
FEAR:

Atheists
Muslims
Homosexuals
Education
Scientists
Humanists
Philosophers
Immigrants
Socialists
Poor people
Rich people
Gun control
Large groups of
black people
The government
Unions
The ACLU
Young people
Liberals
Intellectuals
Hollywood

Why would politicians and presidential hopefuls focus so much attention on Christianity? Because the threat of religious persecution has become an easy way to unify Christian voters and rally them to action.

The same thing happened in the 1970s with the issue of abortion. The Religious Right became one of the most powerful forces in American politics throughout the 1980s, based largely on their opposition to legalized abortion. They essentially handed Republicans control of all three branches of government. A 1980 Harris poll suggested that Jimmy Carter would have defeated Ronald Reagan in the presidential election had it not been for the organization of the Religious Right.

The threat of persecution is one of the most powerful tools for motivating people to action. This threat appeals to our most basic survival instincts. Speaking of his nation's struggle during World War II, Winston Churchill said, "Victory at all costs, victory in spite of all terror, victory however long and hard the road may be; for without victory, there is no survival." Churchill was expressing what every warlord, king, politician, preacher, news pundit, advertiser, and biologist understands: when our survival is at stake, we will fight.

Exploiting Fear

Fear is never a good thing. Even when we think fear is serving us by keeping us out of dangerous situations, such as avoiding the edge of a steep cliff, it is not fear that is helping us at that point but prudence or caution. In fact, fear is the very thing that could do us in at such moments by causing us to doubt ourselves, panic, and unwittingly engineer our own demise.

We see this truth explained especially well in 1 John 4:8.

> There is no fear in love, but perfect love casts out fear; for fear has to do with punishment, and whoever fears has not reached perfection in love.

Fear is especially destructive and offensive when it is used to control others. Fear is at the heart of the persecution complex. Christian communities have been fed a continual diet of reasons to fear others. Fear is the malicious core

Dungeons & Dragons
Change
Artists
Questions
Strong women
Doubt
Astrology
Spirituality
Weakness
Sensuality
Fantasy (unless it's Narnia or Lord of the Rings)
Alcohol
Death
Evolution
Halloween
Santa Claus
Environmentalists
Rock n Roll
Adult cartoons
Pokémon
Harry Potter
Scary movies
Pacifism

of the persecution complex that is used to create community and move people to action.

The Equal Rights Amendment was introduced in 1923. The purpose of this proposed constitutional amendment was to guarantee that women received equal treatment to men in the United States. The ERA fought for recognition and ratification from the 1920s until the 1980s. Support for and opposition to the ERA changed dramatically during this period. The amendment was introduced at every congressional session from 1923 to 1970, although it was usually held up in committee and almost never reached the floor of the House or the Senate for a vote. Most of the opposition to the ERA was centered around its supposed potential effects on the labor market.

The late 1970s and early 1980s saw the most organized opposition to the ERA. Before 1980, the Republican Party had officially supported it, but now opposition to the amendment became important to religious, traditionalist conservatives who were becoming the most influential segment of the Republican Party. Phyllis Schlafly, a conservative lawyer, led the charge to defend traditional gender roles by opposing the ERA.

Together with her peers, Schlafly promoted the idea that women would be drafted into the military and sent into combat (a message that affected many Americans following the Vietnam War). They also told women they would lose their "dependent spouse" status and be forced to use unisex public bathrooms. Their strategy was successful, and the ERA has been officially dead since 1984.

This strategy to defeat the ERA was built on instilling fear in the American public: fear that their traditional values were being undermined, fear that liberal extremists were stealing their freedom, fear of having to use the toilet in mixed company. In short, fear of persecution.

George Smathers was a US senator who represented Florida from 1951 to 1969. During the 1950 election, *Time* magazine reported that Smathers attempted to disparage his opponent during a speech by saying,

> Are you aware that Claude Pepper is known all over Washington as a shameless extrovert? Not only that, but this man is reliably reported to practice nepotism with his sister-in-law, he has a brother who is a known Homo sapien, and he has a sister who was once a thespian in wicked New York. Worst of all, it is an established fact that Mr. Pepper, before his marriage, habitually practiced celibacy.[28]

This speech is now known as the Redneck Speech and is believed to be the creation of a reporter, not of George Smathers. He likely never made such a speech. It is a believable story though, because we understand the propensity of politicians to instill fear in their constituency.

Senator George Smathers with
John F. Kennedy, 1963, Florida Memory

As Christians, we are encouraged not to fear by Bible passages such as 1 John 4:18: "There is no fear in love, but perfect love casts out fear; for fear has to do with punishment, and whoever fears has not reached perfection in love." Yet we are also told, by Christian leaders, that we have much to fear.

Christians throughout America have been convinced they should fear Muslims. This fear turns into opposition to mosques located near our homes. It turns into suspicion that Muslims are secretly trying to subvert our government from within. It turns

American military action in the Middle East into a holy war against the enemies of Christianity.

In 2010, outrage spread across America because of a proposed Islamic center to be built two blocks from the site of the World Trade Center in New York City. That same year a pastor in Florida announced his plan to commemorate 9/11 by burning copies of the Quran. These two examples demonstrate the fear Americans have developed regarding Muslims.

Many Christians have also been convinced they should fear homosexuals. In many ways, Uganda has followed the lead of conservative American Christians. The majority of Uganda's population is Christian, but they still struggle with several challenges, including widespread AIDS. Many American Christian organizations have done significant amounts of work in Uganda, giving aid and spreading the message of Christ. Much of this work has been good, but an unintended consequence has been the imposition of American, conservative values onto a culture that is quite different from America.

The anti-gay attitude that has developed in Uganda is especially dangerous. The Uganda

Politicians promote fear to win elections. Police departments and militaries do it to expand budgets and obtain new powers.

—Daniel Gardner, from *The Science of Fear*

Anti-Homosexuality Act was introduced in 2009. This proposed law would make it illegal to be homosexual, and even initially made provision for a person to be executed for repeated homosexual activity. This legislation was debated for several years and finally passed at the end of 2013 without the inclusion of the death penalty for homosexuals. They would receive life in prison instead. This Anti-Homosexuality Act has been severely criticized by various nations and human rights organizations. It has also been supported by American Evangelical leaders and organizations. Organizations such as the Family Research Council, International House of Prayer, and the American Family Association drew severe criticism for support of the bill.

The Ugandan court struck down the law on August 1, 2014, because it was passed in a parliamentary session that lacked a quorum. The validity of the law will likely be debated for years to come.

American Christians who thought they were encouraging Ugandans to reject immorality have instead exported hatred, fear, false information, and violence. In Uganda, information from discredited conversion therapist Richard A. Cohen was distributed throughout the country stating:

- Homosexuals are at least twelve times more likely to molest children than heterosexuals

- Homosexual teachers are at least seven times more likely to molest a pupil

- Homosexual teachers are estimated to have committed at least 25 percent of pupil molestation

- Forty percent of molestation assaults were made by those who engage in homosexuality[29]

These claims are not only false but also outrageous. They are designed to portray homosexuals as deviants who should be feared, excluded, and punished. Many American Christians are still encouraged to believe such ideas. Religious and political leaders know that fear of dangerous sexual perversion and the devious "gay agenda" can effectively drive people to action.

Fear is a powerful tool used by politicians, advertisers, preachers, and teachers. Fear may be the most effective way to move people to action. Most of the time, though, the object of our fear is only an illusion. The use of fear as motivation is a form of manipulation and exploitation.

8

Persecution Legitimizes Our Cause

"Even today a crude sort of persecution is all that is required to create an honourable name for any sect, no matter how indifferent in itself." Friedrich Nietzsche made this statement in his book *The Anti-Christ*, which is an exhaustive criticism of Christianity. The book was published in 1889, but the statement is just as relevant today as it was then.

The victimization associated with persecution brings not only a sense of community but also a sense of legitimacy to our beliefs and actions. We have a natural tendency to ascribe righteousness to persecuted parties. As Nietzsche said, "a crude sort of persecution is all that is required."

Movies continually take advantage of our tendency to attribute honor to the persecuted. How many of us root for the Jamaican bobsled team in *Cool Runnings*? Of course we do. We see the team as worthy of our support because they are the underdogs. Not only do they face insurmountable odds, but they face the abuse of other teams, sports commentators, and the Olympic governing board.

Numerous other films take advantage of this same inclination for the audience to equate victimization with worthiness: *Forrest Gump, The Shawshank Redemption, Charlie and the Chocolate Factory, Napoleon Dynamite, Finding Nemo*, the *Lord of the Rings* and *Star Wars* series, *Mr. Smith Goes to Washington, It's a Wonderful Life, The Green Mile, Braveheart, The King's Speech, Rocky, Pirates of the Caribbean, Fight Club, The Kid, Up, Apollo 13, Dead Poets Society, Remember the Titans, The Karate Kid...*

FILMS THAT HIGHLIGHT CHRISTIANS' PERSECUTION COMPLEX:

Left Behind (2000)

Left Behind (2014)

Tribulation Force (2002)

A Thief in the Night (1972)

A Distant Thunder (1978)

Image of the Beast (1981)

The Prodigal Planet (1983)

The Omega Code (1999)

Apocalypse (1998)

Apocalypse II (1999)

Authors do it, too. In the Harry Potter series, author J. K. Rowling does not have to take the time to convince us that Harry is worthy of our interest and support. We are immediately convinced of this, because he has been orphaned and is terribly mistreated by his aunt and uncle. Persecution makes Harry honorable.

Claiming that we are being victimized, marginalized, and abused by the powerful says to others, "Our cause is just." Persecution creates legitimacy.

In his 2014 book *God Less America*, Todd Starnes attempts to reveal America's animosity toward Christianity.

The White House is waging an all-out assault on religious liberty. Public schools are indoctrinating our children with the gospel of secularism. Hollywood is spewing toxins into our homes. The soundtrack of our lives is a pulsating mix of sex and violence and filth.[30]

Starnes knows this kind of hysterical language appeals to those who embrace the persecution narrative. His audience reads his books not to be more informed but to feel justified.

Screenwriter John Rogers (*Transformers, Catwoman, Leverage*) says the desire to feel justified via persecution is a fundamental aspect of human nature.

One of the great secrets of human nature is that the one thing people want more than love, security, sex, chocolate or big-screen TV's is to feel hard done by. Why? Because being hard done by is the shit. Feeling hard done by is the sweetest of drugs. If you're being persecuted—it must mean you're doing the right thing, right? You get the mellow buzz of the moral high ground, but without arrogantly claiming it as your own. You get an instant, supportive community in a big dark scary world of such scope it may well literally

Apocalypse III (2000)

Megiddo (2001)

Time Changer (2002)

Six: The Mark Unleashed (2004)

The Moment After (1999)

The Moment After 2 (2006)

The Mark (2012)

God's Not Dead (2014)

Persecuted (2014)

be beyond rational human processing. When you are hard done by, you get purpose in a life where otherwise, you'd have to find your own. And when you ride that high, then no amount of logic, no pointing out that in actuality you and your beliefs are at a high point of popularity and influence for the last hundred years—is going to pry that sweet crack-pipe of moral indignation from your hands.[31]

9

Persecution Gives Us Someone to Blame

I have a garden growing in front of my home. Right now about a dozen tomatoes are ripening. I expect most of them will be ready to eat in a week or so. Last year, my attempt at growing tomatoes yielded one tomato that only grew to about three inches in diameter. I did something wrong. I knew I had to garden differently this year if I actually wanted a bounty of large, juicy tomatoes.

In most areas of our lives, failure indicates that we did something wrong. The persecution complex, however, allows us to lay all the blame for our failures at the feet of our persecutors. This would be the same as blaming last year's poor tomato crop on my neighbor. "All the weeds are not the problem; it's my neighbor who sneaks over in the middle of the night and sprinkles poison on my tomato plants. It's not the fact that I didn't cultivate the soil; it's my tomato-hating neighbor who comes over and tramples the plants while I'm not looking."

If church attendance is declining, we can blame the growing bias against Christians. When our after-school outreach program fails, we can blame anti-Christian policies in public schools. When the values of the culture begin to shift away from the traditional values Christians have held in past generations, we can blame the media's immorality. The persecution narrative says that we are never wrong. The reason we fail is the opposition of secularists and liberals.

> The central belief of every moron is that he is the victim of a mysterious conspiracy against his common rights and true deserts. He ascribes all his failure to get on in the world, all of his congenital incapacity and damfoolishness, to the machinations of werewolves assembled in Wall Street, or some other such den of infamy.
>
> —H. L. Mencken, "Varieties of Envy," from *A Second Mencken Chrestomathy*

We continually hear that we should expect opposition. In his devotional book *Thirst No More*, Dillon Burroughs says, "If we are not receiving some type of ridicule for our beliefs, we are probably doing something wrong."[32] This perspective validates the moral superiority of our position, and we believe that our failures are proof of our righteousness.

This can be a disastrous perspective. The persecution complex prevents us from learning from our mistakes and allows us to justify hurtful, offensive, and damaging behavior toward outsiders as well as people within our communities as we keep a lookout for heretics and other naysayers who may have been infected with society's destructive ideas.

When tempted toward such thinking, we need to adopt the perspective of Thom Rainer, author of *I Am a Church Member.*

> If outside forces and culture were the reasons behind declining and non-influential churches, we would likely have no churches today. The greatest periods of growth, particularly the first-century growth, took place in adversarial cultures. We are not hindered by external forces; we are hindered by our own lack of commitment and selflessness.[33]

PART 3

Why is the Persecution Narrative So Dangerous?

10

Six Damaging Consequences of the Persecution Narrative

The persecution complex has become an integral doctrine of the faith of many American Christians. However, the persecution complex has moved us away from the heart of Jesus and has damaged the ministry of the Christian Church. It is causing Christians to look less like Jesus. We are holding up a distorted image of Jesus and thus a false image of God. As a result, the persecution complex results in six specific damaging consequences.

1. We Feel and Act Superior to Others

The propensity for the idea of persecution to create community, rally us to action, legitimize our cause, and give us someone to blame can very easily cause us to feel superior to others. We are right; everyone else is wrong. We have good ideas; they have bad ideas. We are moral; they are immoral. We are chosen; they are not.

> Our culture is superior. Our culture is superior because our religion is Christianity and that is the truth that makes men free.
>
> —Pat Buchanan

Another contributor to this feeling of superiority is *group polarization*. This is the tendency for a

Let each of you look not to your own interests, but to the interests of others. Let the same mind be in you that was in Christ Jesus, who, though he was in the form of God, did not regard equality with God as something to be exploited, but emptied himself, taking the form of a slave, being born in human likeness. And being found in human form, he humbled himself and became obedient to the point of death— even death on a cross.

Philippians 2:4–8

group of people who agree on a particular topic to become more extreme in their position than they are individually. We see this whenever we get together with others who are like-minded politically, morally, or religiously. It is a dynamic that exerts itself at dinner parties and political rallies. The phenomenon of group polarization can be especially potent when we begin to talk about persecution.

The persecution complex really only exists within large groups. Individual Christians are generally kind, accepting, gracious, and humble. When Christians get together in groups and are influenced to believe they are oppressed, it is then that they become aggressive, rude, judgmental, and arrogant. Group polarization feeds the sense of superiority that can easily exist in Christian groups who claim persecution.

Author Candida Moss writes about historic Christian martyrdom and its effects on our current ideas about persecution in her book *The Myth of Persecution: How Early Christians Invented a Story of Martyrdom*. Moss asserts that our understanding of the persecution of the early church is terribly exaggerated. I disagree with her conclusions about historic persecution and martyrdom, but I wholeheartedly agree with her thoughts about contemporary ideas of persecution. She says,

The myth of Christian martyrdom and persecution needs to be corrected, because it has left us with a dangerous legacy that poisons the well of public discourse. This affects not just Christians, but everyone. We cannot use the mere fact that we feel persecuted as evidence that our cause is just or as the grounds for rhetorical or actual war. We cannot use the supposed moral superiority of our ancient martyrs to demonstrate the intrinsic superiority of our modern religious beliefs or ideological positions. Once we recognize that feeling persecuted is not proof of anything, then we have to engage in serious intellectual and moral debate about the actual issues at hand.[34]

Jesus never exhibited an air of superiority. He was humble unto death. For us to be people who demonstrate the character of Jesus, we must not imagine that we are better than the "other."

2. We Justify Antagonism

The sacrificial example of Jesus says to turn the other cheek, walk the extra mile, love our enemies, refuse to resist an evil person, and give up our desires to the point of death.

The persecution narrative complex says our faith is under assault and must be defended. It says we are the good guys while the secularists and liberals are

"You have heard that it was said, 'An eye for an eye and a tooth for a tooth.' But I say to you, Do not resist an evildoer. But if anyone strikes you on the right cheek, turn the other also; and if anyone wants to sue you and take your coat, give your cloak as well; and if anyone forces you to go one mile, go also the second mile. Give to everyone who begs from you, and do not refuse anyone who wants to borrow from you.

"You have heard that it was said, 'You shall love your neighbor and hate your enemy.' But I say to you, Love your enemies and pray for those who persecute you, so that you may be children of your Father in heaven; for he makes his sun rise on the evil and on the good, and sends rain on the righteous and on the unrighteous. For if you love those who love you, what reward do you have? Do not even the tax collectors do the same? And if you greet only your brothers and sisters, what more are you doing than others? Do not even the Gentiles do the same? Be perfect, therefore, as your heavenly Father is perfect."

Matthew 5:38–48

the bad guys. And it says we should never back down, never defer, never give an inch, and never allow our opposition to offend us without being challenged.

Sometimes Christians say the peaceful teachings of Jesus do not apply to all situations. Admittedly, it is very difficult to apply "turn the other cheek" (Matthew 5:39) to foreign relations, but Jesus never qualifies his teaching. He never says it applies to certain situations, but not others. He never says some people should apply principles of peace, forgiveness, and non-violence, but others should not.

Many of us have accepted the idea that Jesus was asking human beings to behave a certain way, but that God is above these behavioral restrictions. It is likely that we justify our antagonistic attitudes because we actually believe God is antagonistic toward humans. If God hates those people, then we should be allowed to hate them, too. If God wants to punish them for their animosity toward God's self, then we are perfectly justified is hoping for the same. Jesus addressed this in his teaching, though. In Matthew 5:44–45, after he has talked about forgiveness, loving one's enemies, and not judging, he says, "But I say to you, Love your enemies and pray for those who persecute you, so that you may be children of your Father in heaven; for he makes his sun rise on the evil and on the good, and sends rain on the righteous and on the unrighteous."

When Jesus says, "So that you may be children of your Father in heaven," he is saying the behaviors he has described are the ways the Father behaves. A child of the Father is like the Father. God the Father forgives even when God has been treated wrongly; so should God's children. God the Father loves God's enemies; so should God's children. Jesus is correcting the idea that God is vindictive or retributive. When Jesus says, "He makes his sun rise on the evil and on the good, and sends rain on the righteous and on the unrighteous," he is saying God's blessings come to everyone. He is correcting the idea that God treats some people well while punishing others.

Developing an antagonistic relationship with those with whom we disagree is very easy, but if we want to be children of God and followers of Jesus, we must choose to see no one as our enemy. If the persecution narrative brings antagonism, then we are obliged by the teachings of Jesus to reject it.

3. We Dehumanize Others

The persecution narrative and the culture war often turn people into issues: The gay issue, the environmental issue, the contraception issue, the abortion issue...

If we look back into history for the character of present sects in Christianity, we shall find few that have not in their turns been persecutors, and complainers of persecution. The primitive Christians thought persecution extremely wrong in the Pagans, but practised it on one another. The first Protestants of the Church of England, blamed persecution in the Roman church, but practised it against the Puritans: these found it wrong in the Bishops, but fell into the same practice themselves both here and in New England.

—Benjamin Franklin, Letter to the *London Packet*, June 3, 1772

I grew up in the conservative Evangelical world, where I learned to stand up for "biblical truth" on each of these issues, as well as many others. It was easy for me to toe the party line regarding homosexuality until a friend of mine told me he was gay and how he continued to struggle to force himself to be straight because he was afraid of going to hell. It is easy to see abortion as an issue to stand against until you know a young woman who is raped and feels she simply cannot force herself to bring a child into the world in which she lives. It is easy to stand up for business, capitalism, and the job-creating energy companies until you see the devastation to the health of the poor that has been wrought in coal mining communities. It is easy to stand against the "war on Christmas" until you have a Muslim friend who tells you of the loneliness and exclusion she feels between Halloween and New Year's Day.

When the human problems of our society are reduced to issues on which we must take a stand, then we easily lose sight of the people who are struggling, hurting, and in need of grace and love. Taking a stand causes us to see those with whom we disagree as the enemy and those caught in the middle of our debate as people to be converted or defeated.

4. We Eliminate Conversation and Debate

Viewing another person as the "other," or especially as the enemy, allows us to dismiss their perspective as invalid.

In 2011, superstar pastor Rob Bell released the book *Love Wins*. In his book Bell supported the idea that ultimate reconciliation (everyone eventually goes to heaven) may be more consistent with the character of God than Evangelicalism's prevalent doctrine of atonement, which says a majority of humanity will end up in hell. Even though Bell's ideas about heaven and hell were not new to some segments of Christianity, they were shocking to Evangelicals. *Love Wins* set off an explosion of questions, books, sermons, and discussions about hell at churches all across America. The book also gave many Evangelical leaders the verification that Rob Bell is a heretic and a false teacher. Another superstar pastor, John Piper, made his now famous tweet, "Farewell Rob Bell."

Rob Bell was now outside the camp of acceptable doctrine, and John Piper, along with thousands of other Evangelical Christians, were dismissing everything Bell had ever taught. Zondervan would no longer publish his books, and Lifeway Christian stores would no longer sell his products. A pastor even told me he would not be using resources from New Testament scholar Ray Vander Laan, because Vander Laan was once associated with Rob Bell.

When Rob Bell became the enemy of conservative Evangelicalism, all of his teaching and ideas were dismissed. A few years earlier, Bell had been a hero of Evangelicals because of his creative communication, his insightful exegesis of Scripture, and his rapidly growing church. None of that mattered anymore.

When a person is identified as the enemy, nothing they say to us matters. Their perspective, experiences, and ideas are invalidated. This eliminates any chance of relationship or reconciliation.

This is exactly what happens when we view certain people or groups as our persecutors. They become our enemies and, therefore, unworthy of our respect. We find their concerns, experiences, values, and priorities invalid. We don't have to listen to them, and we certainly don't have to love them.

This is not only selfish and antagonistic, it is anti-Christ.

5. We Become Immune to Criticism

Since persecution gives us someone to blame (chapter 6), it also allows us to reject any criticism laid on us. We can choose not to accept the blame for our failures, but we can also choose not to accept criticism of our actions or attitudes. Christians have often been accused of being rude, arrogant, judgmental, and homophobic. The persecution complex allows us to attribute any of these criticisms to anti-Christian bias.

When someone calls us hypocritical, we can say they are projecting their own problem on us. If they call us rude and arrogant, we can blame it on their prejudice against Christians. If we are called homophobic and hateful, we can say that our accusers refuse to accept biblical truth.

In the book *unChristian*, authors David Kinnaman and Gabe Lyons of the Barna Research Group identify six negative perceptions non-Christians have of Christians: hypocritical, uncaring, anti-homosexual, sheltered, too political, and judgmental.[35] Their book, *unChristian*, is a fairly harsh indictment of Christians in America. If we take these six accusations seriously, then we need to make some adjustments in the way we live out Christianity.

Yet, it is very easy for us to dismiss the observations of Kinnaman and Lyons as being based on the opinions of people who are unjustifiably hostile to Christianity. We could easily say, "Of course they don't like us; they didn't like Jesus." That is not the way Jesus would respond, though. That is not the way of humility.

A 2010 article in the *Journal of Experimental Psychology* claimed victimization is the most effective way of deflecting blame. "In situations where people (or their lawyers) seek to escape blame for wrongdoing, they often use one of two strategies: frame themselves as a hero (hero strategy) or as a victim (victim strategy). The hero strategy acknowledges wrongdoing but highlights previous good deeds to offset blame. The victim strategy also acknowledges wrongdoing but highlights the harms suffered by the perpetrator to deflect blame." Authors Kurt Gray and Daniel Wegner go on to explain, "Three studies found that victim strategy consistently reduced blame, while the hero strategy was at best ineffectual and at worst harmful. This effect appeared to stem from how the minds of victims and heroes are perceived."[36]

Then the righteous will answer him, "Lord, when was it that we saw you hungry and gave you food, or thirsty and gave you something to drink? And when was it that we saw you a stranger and welcomed you, or naked and gave you clothing? And when was it that we saw you sick or in prison and visited you?"

Dinesh D'Souza's campaign finance troubles demonstrate this desire to deflect blame by claiming persecution. In a Fox News interview with Megyn Kelly on September 23, 2014, D'Souza said, "My own country tried to put me away and the court said no."

The following day, D'Souza indicated to *The Daily Caller* that he had been targeted by Eric Holder and the Justice Department.[37] Dinesh D'Souza's refusal to accept responsibility for his crimes is a prime indication of a persecution complex.

6. We Ignore the Real Problems of Human Suffering

Many religious and political leaders characterize anti-Christian persecution in America as a dire problem requiring our undivided attention. In a July 2014 article recounting religious hostility in America, David Barton said, "Many of these actions are literally unprecedented—this is the first time they have happened in four centuries of American history. The hostility of President Obama toward Biblical faith and values is without equal from any previous American president."[38]

Books, blogs, magazine articles, and Sunday morning sermons often ascribe such urgency to the problem of persecution that it seems to be the only issue worthy of our attention.

I was once part of organizing home groups within a small church. These were mid-week meetings that took place at the homes of various church members. The groups gave members an opportunity to discuss

And the king will answer them, "Truly I tell you, just as you did it to one of the least of these who are members of my family, you did it to me."

Matthew 25:37–40

spiritual issues in a more intimate, casual setting than at church on Sunday morning. We decided to ask each group to adopt a nation. They would spend a little bit of time each week learning about this country and praying for its needs. This would help those attending the groups to understand the needs of others around the world and to develop a caring heart for people outside the United States. This worked well except for on particular home group leader. He said he simply could not choose a country outside the United States, because he thought America was in such desperate need.

When we come to believe that our own problems, and the needs of America, are the most desperate, we lose sight of the needs of the world. When we magnify the problem of anti-Christian persecution, we minimize issues not related to persecution.

Many Christians have become obsessed with finding instances of Christian persecution. I know a woman who is always ready to point out persecution. Nearly every conversation with her lands in the realm of politics and the oppression of Christians in the United States. Once, at a backyard picnic, she warned the group of us that some of the food might be poisoned. "Liberals trying to get rid of the Christians," she said. I'm not sure if she was joking or not.

Anxiety over persecution tends to take precedence over every other issue. Continually being on the lookout for Christian persecution distracts us from concern about hunger, abuse, poverty, and the issues about which Jesus told his followers to be concerned. Jesus had a lot to say about the way his followers treated others. He talked about their care for the hungry and helpless. Never once though did he tell his disciples to fight for religious freedom or to stand up for what they believed.

When we fall for the persecution complex, not only do we overlook the real suffering of so many other people in the world, we also become blinded to the kinds of suffering we create through our self-centered addiction to fear.

The Persecution Complex vs. Jesus

Persecuted Christian	Jesus
Feels superior to those who believe or live differently	Is the servant of all
Stands up for his/her beliefs	Lays down his life
Is willing to malign and mistreat her/his political or religious opponents	Loves his enemies and does not resist an evil person
Says the world is a battle ground	The world is full of people who need direction and love
Does not associate with those of differing moral values or religious doctrine	Spends time with and enjoys the company of those with questionable character and lifestyles
Desires positions of power and influence	Stands with those at the margins of society
Is offended when his or her religion is marginalized	Is offended by the withholding of justice and mercy
Is positioned against those with moral failings	Is positioned as an ally of those with moral failings
Delights n the destruction of his or her enemies	Asks God to forgive His enemies
Compiles books, web sites, films, and articles that recount the behavior of his/her enemies	Keeps no record of wrong
Defends doctrine and tradition	Defends people
Believes the world is on the brink of destruction	Says the kingdom of God is at hand
Believes God punishes	Believes God forgives

PART 4

How Can We Break Away From the Persecution Narrative?

11

An Honest Look Toward Change

The persecution complex will continue to damage our ability to bring the love of Jesus to the world unless we choose to make changes to the way we relate to people and to the expectations we have of the world around us. Here are some ideas about how we can do this.

Do People Like Us?

Many times we are treated badly because of "some notion of our own." We call this *persecution* and say things like, "Of course they don't like us. They didn't like Jesus." This is not true though. People loved Jesus. They flocked to him, traveled great distances, went without food, battled crushing crowds, and even tore holes through roofs to see him. Jesus was loved by the common people. The only people who hated him were the religious and secular authorities who felt threatened by his popularity.

This is a sharp contrast to today, when the powerful establishment loves Christians but common people do not. The establishment likes us, because we

"At heart men are antagonistic to the lordship of Jesus Christ. It is not antagonism to creeds or points of view, but antagonism encountered for My sake. Many of us awaken antagonism by our way of stating things; we have to distinguish between being persecuted for some notion of our own and being persecuted "for My sake."

-Oswald Chambers

127

bring votes and money, and we don't disrupt the system too much. The people don't like us, because they see us as judgmental and continually trying to get them to join our religious club.

He entered Jericho and was passing through it. A man was there named Zacchaeus; he was a chief tax collector and was rich. He was trying to see who Jesus was, but on account of the crowd he could not, because he was short in stature. So he ran ahead and climbed a sycamore tree to see him, because he was going to pass that way. When Jesus came to the place, he looked up and said to him, "Zacchaeus, hurry and come down; for I must stay at your house today." So he hurried down and was happy to welcome him. All who saw it began to grumble and said, "He has

Several years ago, I was in a Target store browsing the movies. There was also another young man in the same area looking through the DVDs. He asked me if I'd seen any good movies lately. This was bit strange. Most of us spend our shopping trips in silence, not engaging anyone. The young man and I talked a little bit about recent movies. He was an engaging person. It was pleasant to talk to someone in the store about something in which I was interested.

Then the conversation changed suddenly. He took out a business card and told me he was looking for enthusiastic people who could join him in a business venture. He asked if he might call me and set up a time when we could meet.

I smiled and said, "Sure," but I was terribly disappointed. I thought he was actually interested in me. I thought he wanted to be my friend, but really, he just wanted to recruit me.

I think that is exactly what some people think when they encounter a Christian. "I thought you were actually interested in me. I thought you wanted to be my friend, but, really, you just want me to buy your religion."

How different this is from the story of Jesus' engagement with Zacchaeus in the Gospel of Luke. Zacchaeus was so excited to see Jesus that he found out the route Jesus was taking through Jericho and climbed a tree so he could see Him over the heads of the crowds. When Jesus spotted Zacchaeus, He invited himself to Zacchaeus's home.

This is incredible, because Zacchaeus was a tax collector. He would have been viewed as a person who was loyal to Rome and a traitor to his own people. He was wealthy, somewhat powerful, but despised by most of his neighbors.

gone to be the guest of one who is a sinner." Zacchaeus stood there and said to the Lord, "Look, half of my possessions, Lord, I will give to the poor; and if I have defrauded anyone of anything, I will pay back four times as much." Then Jesus said to him, "Today salvation has come to this house, because he too is a son of Abraham. For the Son of Man came to seek out and to save the lost."

Luke 19:1–10

Jesus never preached to Zacchaeus or told him to change his ways. When Zacchaeus experienced the acceptance and love of Jesus, though, he immediately promised to repay anyone he had cheated and to give half his wealth to the poor. How often does our simple example of love and acceptance inspire others to do the same? I can't help but think that we would be more likely to picket the man's home in order to shame him into changing his ways.

The Prophetic Voice

Prophets are often misunderstood. Pop culture and bad theology have given us the idea that prophecy is simply a prediction of the future, often delivered by a strangely mystical person, frequently in some sort of riddle.

The biblical prophet is quite different from this. The Old Testament contains seventeen books that are considered prophecy. These are books written by prophets of the ancient nation of Israel. The biblical prophet is one who brings a message from God. Biblical prophets are often confrontational and are frequently bringing their message to authorities and people of power. Old Testament prophets point out the ways the nation has strayed from God, and they call the people to return to God. They convict leaders of their idolatry, their neglect of the poor and helpless, their empty religiosity, and their greed, pride, and violence. The prophets declare that destruction will occur if people continue on the wrong path, and they imagine a better world if people choose to follow God's way. The prophet's message is especially relevant to leaders and people of power. The prophet speaks truth to power.

Prophets, including Jesus, were often despised, run out of town, and killed by the authorities of their time. People in power rarely like prophets, but prophets are necessary.

America needs prophets: not prophets who call out the evils of homosexuality and abortion and predict the end of days but prophets who expose the evils of greed, war, poverty, and racial inequity. Prophets who will confront the injustice of the American penal system. Prophets who will stand up to corporations, addressing their greed, abuse of the poor, and neglect of the planet.

America needs prophets who will address the system of violence used to guard American interests at the expense of the innocent. Prophets who will advocate on behalf of the poor trapped by systems of inequality that benefit some while neglecting others. America needs prophets who will expose the systemic racism that still marginalizes African-Americans, Latinos, Asians, Native Americans, and other racial minorities. Prophets who will stand against the exploitation of the earth for convenience and economic gain. Prophets who will speak out about the excess and abuse of the religious industrial complex in America.

Prophets stand with the marginalized and speak to the powerful. They willingly identify with the suffering. Prophets do not seek positions of power for themselves, but they seek to influence the powerful.

Fighting Injustice Rather Than Persecution

American Christians are not experiencing persecution because they are the prophetic voice of truth to the powerful. We believe we are persecuted because persecution benefits us. The persecution complex causes us to continually be on the lookout for the next offense. It makes us sensitive and defensive. We become guarded and suspicious. The persecution complex is selfish.

I believe the solution is to turn our attention to the defense of other needy, abused, and marginalized people rather than focusing on our own abuse and marginalization. We must stop looking for persecution and open our eyes to injustice.

Persecution is an offense against our religion. Injustice is an offense against the humanity of another person. We should recognize that Jesus never stood up for his religion. He never attempted to defend himself from the persecution of others. He did stand up for justice and the righteous treatment of others. He did encourage his followers to defend and provide for the orphan, the widow, and the stranger, helpless people who were in need of a provider and an advocate.

"Then the king will say to those at his right hand, 'Come, you that are blessed by my Father, inherit the kingdom prepared for you from the foundation of the world; for I was hungry and you gave me food, I was thirsty and you gave me something to drink, I was a stranger and you welcomed me, I was naked and you gave me clothing, I was sick and you took care of me, I was in prison and you visited me.' Then the righteous will answer him, 'Lord, when was it that we saw you hungry and gave you food, or thirsty and gave you something to drink?

Today, 780 million people live without access to clean water. That is two and a half times the population of the United States. Another 3.4 million people die each year from water-related disease. Every twenty-one seconds a child dies due to a water-related illness.[39] This is an injustice that needs our attention.

Around 21,000 children die each day due to poverty. Four million newborns die each year before their first month of life. Over 500,000 women die each year due to complications from pregnancy and childbirth.[40] These are injustices we should be concerned about.

More than one of every 100 American adults is in prison, the majority for nonviolent crimes. The number of black males in prison is nearly ten times greater than the number of white males.[41] About 75 percent of those released from prison are arrested again within five years.[42] The American prison system is a rapidly growing industry, not because crime is on the rise but because many people benefit from this system. This is an injustice about which we should be speaking.

Worldwide, 1.6 billion people live in substandard housing. The number of people living in urban

And when was it that we saw you a stranger and welcomed you, or naked and gave you clothing? And when was it that we saw you sick or in prison and visited you?' And the king will answer them, 'Truly I tell you, just as you did it to one of the least of these who are members of my family, you did it to me.' Then he will say to those at his left hand, 'You that are accursed, depart from me into the eternal fire prepared for the devil and his angels; for I was hungry and you gave me no food, I was thirsty and you gave me nothing to drink, I was a stranger and you did not welcome me, naked and you did not give me clothing, sick and in prison and you did not visit me.' Then they also will answer, 'Lord,

when was it
that we saw you
hungry or thirsty
or a stranger or
naked or sick or
in prison, and
did not take care
of you?' Then
he will answer
them, 'Truly I tell
you, just as you
did not do it to
one of the least
of these, you did
not do it to me.'"

Matthew 25:34-
45

slums is 827.6 million. The percentage of the world's population that lives in unhealthy and unsafe conditions is rising.[43] This is injustice.

An estimated 1.3 million women are victims of physical abuse by an intimate partner each year. Boys who witness domestic violence are twice as likely to abuse their own partners and children when they become adults. Statistics show that 30–60 percent of perpetrators of intimate partner violence also abuse children in the household.[44] Domestic abuse has often been implicitly tolerated in conservative Christian circles. This is injustice.

Nearly 16 million children in America live with the reality of not having enough food. And 22 percent of the children in America live in poverty. One in three African-American children live with food insecurity. Hungry children do poorly in school, leading to fewer opportunities as they grow older.[45] Each year, Americans throw away 33 million tons of food. This is injustice.

When we look at the destructive forces at work around our world, the issue of Christian persecution does not seem quite so important. Turning our attention outward helps us to put

134

things in the right perspective. Standing against our own persecution is to stand up for ourselves. Standing against injustice is to stand up for others—this is the way of Jesus.

In Matthew 25, Jesus gives a parable about the judgment of humanity. This parable has a bit a surprise ending, because Jesus explains that it is not lots of religious activity or adherence to particular points of doctrine that pleases God. It is feeding the poor, clothing the needy, and caring for the sick. Justice pleases God.

Loving Our Enemies

The term "go the extra mile" has become a part of our cultural lexicon, but it originates with Jesus. First century Israel was occupied by Rome, so in addition to the Jewish law, Israelites were bound by Roman law. Roman soldiers were allowed to recruit the help of any resident of an occupied nation. This person could be required to carry the soldier's equipment for one mile, but not more than one mile. This aided the Roman military but kept residents from being abused.

In Jesus' Sermon on the Mount (Matthew 5–7), he has a lot to say about the way His listeners treated their enemies. In Matthew 5:41, Jesus says, "If anyone forces you to go one mile, go also the second mile." Jesus is instructing his followers on how they should treat their hated Roman occupiers. They were obligated by law to go the first mile, but not the second. No one would ever dream of going a second mile. Going a second mile would be giving up ground to their persecutors.

The first mile is required. The second mile is a choice. The first mile is imposed upon me. The second mile requires me to give up my own desires in favor of my enemy. The second mile is transformative. The second mile requires me to give up my victimhood status. During the first mile, I can gripe, complain, and slander my persecutor. During the second mile, I must lay down all my negativity and hatred. The second mile transforms my position from contentious to relational. To go the second mile I cannot stand my ground or fight for my rights.

Whether our persecution is real or contrived, the teaching of Jesus compels us to treat our persecutor with kindness, humility, and love; preferring them above our own needs and desires.

Laying Down Our Lives

"No one has greater love than this, to lay down one's life for one's friends." These are the words of Jesus recorded in John 15:13. We should note the things Jesus did not say. He did not say ...

"No one has greater love than this, to fight for your freedom."

"No one has greater love than this, to send jets to bomb your enemies."

"No one has greater love than this, to pass laws preferring your religion."

"No one has greater love than this, to protest in front of Congress."

"No one has greater love than this, to stand up for your rights."

The example of Jesus is that of non-violent self-sacrifice. His way of giving until his last breath ultimately exposes his enemies, who would oppose him with strength and violence, as impotent. When the soldier at the cross said, "Surely, this man was the son of God," he was seeing that the might of Rome, which crushed Jesus and ended his life, was actually empty. Jesus' way of peace and humility is what truly held power.

When we protest, bring lawsuits, write books, and go to the media to claim that our religion is under attack, we are taking up the weapons of the world rather than following the peaceful way of Jesus. Laying down our lives means that we give ourselves wholly to the needs of those around us. We do not demand that they cater to us.

If then there is any encouragement in Christ, any consolation from love, any sharing in the Spirit, any compassion and sympathy, make my joy complete: be of the same mind, having the same love, being in full accord and of one mind. Do nothing from selfish ambition or conceit, but in humility regard others as better than yourselves. Let each of you look not to your own interests, but to the interests of others. Let the same mind be in you that was in Christ Jesus,

who, though he was in the form of God,
did not regard equality with God
as something to be exploited,
but emptied himself,
taking the form of a slave,
being born in human likeness.
And being found in human form,
he humbled himself
and became obedient to the point of death—
even death on a cross.
Therefore God also highly exalted him and
gave him the name
that is above every name,
so that at the name of Jesus
every knee should bend,

in heaven and on earth and under the earth,
and every tongue should confess
that Jesus Christ is Lord,
to the glory of God the Father.

(Philippians 2:1–11)

May you be a personification of Jesus to the world around you, not claiming persecution but standing for those who are weak and in need; not claiming the position of the victim, but willingly laying down your life for the good of the world.

Amen.

Discussion Guide

Introduction

- In your experience, how has Christian culture promoted the idea that Christians are persecuted?

- Why do some Christians identify certain people—atheists, liberals, homosexuals, etc.—as persecutors or enemies?

- Do you have any experiences in which your opinion of a particular group or person changed after getting to know them?

Chapter 1

- Can you identify with the persecution narrative described in the section "The Script of Persecution?"

- Do you believe that there are similarities between the way some Evangelicals understand persecution and psychological delusion?

- The section "What if We Are Wrong?" begins with the statement, "The persecution narrative can only exist in an environment of pride, because, it is completely self-centered." In what ways has American Christianity been an environment of pride?

· What are some healthy ways to rewrite the script of persecution?

Chapter 2

· Do you believe American Christians are mistreated for the sake of Christ, or for other reasons?

· What reasons could people have for mistreating Christians?

· In what instances is enduring persecution seen as a virtue in our culture?

· Did this chapter alter your understanding of the book of Revelation? How?

· Would you consider yourself a Christian fundamentalist? Why or why not?

· Do you consider patriotism to be a Christian value?

· In what ways has the culture war influenced American society and American Christianity?

· The section "A Fictitious Conflict" states, "If there ever has been a culture war, we have already won." How do you feel about this idea?

· Who do you see benefitting from the persecution narrative?

Chapter 3

· In what way has Christianity enjoyed a position of privilege in American society?

· Is change in that position of privilege good or bad? Why?

· Is consideration for other religions a compromise of Christian convictions?

· Should Christianity ever be positioned in opposition to science?

- What damage has been caused by making homosexuality an issue rather than seeing homosexuals as people?

- How have you experienced the person who claims persecution becoming the persecutor?

Chapter 4

- Does opposition to your beliefs ever cause you to become more entrenched in those beliefs?

- What are some ways that you enjoy familiarity and certainly?

- What problems are caused by longing for the past and being pessimistic about the future?

- When have you experience the instability caused by your sense of certainty slipping away?

Chapter 5

- What are some examples (like that of the road rage

epidemic) of the feedback loop created by media hype exaggerating a story or issue?

· What sources are reinforcing the idea that anti-Christian persecution is a problem?

· Have you ever heard stories of persecution which you found out later where exaggerated or untrue?

Chapter 6

· What are some examples of oppression creating a sense of community?

· What groups (or individuals) become the scapegoats for societal problems?

· What is a time that you have tried to identify yourself as a victim because it would benefit you?

Chapter 7

· Who do you see using fear to drive people to action?

- When have you been motivated to action by fear?

- What damage is done when powerful people use fear as a motivator?

Chapter 8

- When have you identified with the underdog because their disadvantaged position seems to make them attractive?

- Do you ever listen to those who encourage your position as a victim because it makes you feel justified?

Chapter 9

- Who do you see blaming their own failures on the opposition of others?

- When have you blamed your own failure on others?

- In what areas do Christians avoid responsibility by blaming persecutors?

Chapter 10

· What problems are created when we feel superior to others?

· In what ways do antagonistic Christians effect people's view of God?

· Does standing for truth conflict with compassion for people?

· Is it healthy to engage perspective that conflict with our own?

· Do you ever dismiss the criticism of others by placing them in a category that makes their opinion invalid?

· Of what problems can Christians lose sight when viewing persecution as the most urgent problem?

· What problems can American Christians create "through our self-centered addiction to fear?"

· Does the chart at the end of chapter 10 affect your view of Jesus? How?

Chapter 11

· Do you believe that Christians are liked by the whole of American society? What about Evangelicals? Fundamentalists? The Religious Right?

· Can you identify anyone who is acting as a prophet as defined in this chapter; shining light on injustice and speaking truth to power without seeking power?

· Was Jesus persecuted? Why or why not?

· Do any of the injustices listed in this chapter resonate with you?

· Can we love our enemies while standing against persecution?

· Can we lay down our lives while standing against persecution?

Notes

Chapter 1

[1]"John F. Nash, Jr. – Biographical," Nobel Foundation. 1994. http://www.nobelprize.org/nobel_prizes/economic-sciences/laureates/1994/nash-bio.html

[2]John Piper, *Jesus: The Only Way to God: Must You Hear the Gospel to Be Saved?* (Grand Rapids, MI: Baker Books, 2010), 7.

[3]"Persecution Complex: The Religious Right's Deceptive Rallying Cry," People for the American Way, May 21, 2014 http://www.pfaw.org/sites/default/files/upload/persecution_report_V2.pdf

[4]"What I Learned About Atheists from *God's Not Dead*," http://www.patheos.com/blogs/godlessindixie/2014/08/05/what-i-learned-about-atheists-from-gods-not-dead/.

Chapter 2

[5]Oswald Chambers, *The Pilgrim's Song* . (Simpkin Marshall, Ltd. Rossmore Court, Park Road, London, N.W.I. 1941), chap. 4.

[6]John Dickson, *Humilitas: A Lost Key to Life, Love, and Leadership* (Grand Rapids, MI: Zondervan, 2011), 72, 91.

[7]Jonathan Mahler, "Dsouza Avoids Prison Time in Campaign Finance Case," New York Times. September 23, 2014. http://www.nytimes.com/2014/09/24/us/dsouza-is-spared-prison-time-for-campaign-finance-violations.html?_r=2

Chapter 3

[8]"'Nones' on the Rise," Pew Research Center, October 9, 2012 http://www.pewforum.org/Unaffiliated/nones-on-the-rise.aspx

[9]"Scientists and Belief," The Pew Research Center, November 5, 2009 http://www.pewforum.org/2009/11/05/scientists-and-belief/

[10]Faith & Liberty, July 23, 2014 http://www.ohiochristian.edu/faith-liberty/podcast/michele-bachmann-direction-nation-andrew-mccarthy-why-president-should-be-impe

[11]"Sexual Identity, Sex of Sexual Contacts, and Health-Risk Behaviors Among Students in Grades 9-12: Youth Risk Behavior Surveillance," CDC,. Atlanta, GA: U.S. Department of Health and Human Services, 2011.

[12]"The Role of Help-Seeking in Preventing Suicide Attempts among Lesbians, Gay Men, and Bisexuals," Ilan H. Meyer PhD, Merilee Yeylan MPH, Sharin Scwartz PhD. The American Association of Suicidology, May 14, 2014.

Chapter 4

[13]"On Alcohol Use in America," http://www.sbc.net/resolutions/1156.

[14]Steven Pressfield, *The War of Art: Break Through the Blocks and Win Your Inner Creative Battles* (New York, NY: Black Irish Entertainment, 2002), 35.

[15]Robert A. Burton, MD, *On Being Certain: Believing You Are Right Even When You're Not* (New York, NY: St. Martin's Press, 2008), from the Preface.

[16]Ibid, 88.

[17]David Rock, "A Hunger for Certainty." *Psychology Today,* October 25, 2009 http://www.psychologytoday.com/blog/your-brain-work/200910/hunger-certainty

Chapter 5

[18]Matthew L. Wald, "Temper Cited as Cause of 28,000 Road Deaths a Year," *Time,* July 18, 1997. http://www.nytimes.com/1997/07/18/us/temper-cited-as-cause-of-28000-road-deaths-a-year.html

[19]Daniel Gardner, *The Science of Fear: Why We Fear the Things We Shouldn't—and Put Ourselves in Greater Danger* (New York, NY: Penguin Group, Inc. 2008), 177.

[20]Neil Genzlinger, "They're Out to Get Him, Whoever They Are," *New York Times,* July 17, 2014. http://www.nytimes.com/2014/07/18/movies/persecuted-focuses-on-a-tv-evangelist.html?&_r=1

[21]Annie Murphy Paul, "Your Brain Fiction," *New York Times,* March 17, 2012. http://www.nytimes.com/2012/03/18/opinion/sunday/the-neuroscience-of-your-brain-on-fiction.html?pagewanted=all

[22]Daniel Gardner, *The Science of Fear: How the Culture of Fear Manipulates Your* Brain (New York, NY: Penguin Group, 2008), 180.

Chapter 6

[23]Ta-Nehsis Coates, "The NAACP Is Right." *The Atlantic,* June 15, 2010. http://www.theatlantic.com/national/archive/2010/07/the-naacp-is-right/59793/

[24]The ideas of communal violence and scapegoating are brilliantly organized in mimetic theory, developed by twentieth century philosopher Rene Girard. His books *The Scapegoat, Violence and the Sacred,* and *I See Satan Fall Like Lightening* (among his many works) reveal these ideas especially well.

[25]"'Nones' on the Rise," Pew Research Center, October 9, 2012. http://www.pewforum.org/Unaffiliated/nones-on-the-rise.aspx

[26]Victor Luckerson, "How Nonprofits Convince Millennials to Give: Customize the Cause." *Time,* December 27, 2012. http://business.time.com/2012/12/27/how-nonprofits-convince-millennials-to-give-customize-the-cause/.

Chapter 7
[27]FRC Action videos from the Values Voters Summit https://www.youtube.com/FRCAction/videos
[28]"FLORIDA: Anything Goes." *Time* 55 (16), April 17, 1950.
[29]Richard A. Cohen, *Coming Out Straight: Understanding and Healing Homosexuality* (Winchester, VA: Oakhill Press, 2000), 49.

Chapter 8
[30]Todd Starnes, *God Less America,* (Lake Mary, FL: Charisma House Book Group, 2014), 3.
[31]John Rogers, "'Toxic Spiritual Nature' … and Those Desks Pinch." Kung Fu Monkey. June 2, 2005. http://kfmonkey.blogspot.com/2005/06/toxic-spiritual-nature-and-those-desks.html

Chapter 9
[32]Dillon Burroughs, *Thirst No More: A One-Year Devotional Journey* (Birmingham, AL: New Hope Publishers, 2011), chap. "April 13."
[33]Thom S. Rainer, *I Am a Church Member: Discovering the Attitude that Makes the Difference* (Nashville, TN: B&H Books, 2013), chap. 1.

Chapter 10
[34]Candida Moss, *The Myth of Persecution: How Early Christians Invented a Story of Martyrdom.* (New York, NY: Harper Collins Publishers, 2013), 256.
[35]David Kinnaman and Gabe Lyons, *unChristian: What a New Generation Really Thinks about Christianity…and Why It Matters,* (Grand Rapids, MI: Baker Books, 2007).
[36]Kurt Gray and Daniel M. Wegner, "To Escape Blame, Don't Be a Hero—Be a Victim," *Journal of Experimental Psychology,* Volume 47, Issue 2, March 2011.
[37]Luke Brinker, "Dinesh D'Souza's pathetic persecution complex: No, he isn't the victim of a government conspiracy!" *Salon,* September 24, 2014. http://www.salon.com/2014/09/24/dinesh_d%E2%80%99souza%E2%80%99s_pathetic_persecution_complex_no_he_isn%E2%80%99t_the_victim_of_a_government_conspiracy/
[38]David Barton, "America's Most Biblically-Hostile U.S. President," Wall Builders, July 8, 2014. http://www.wallbuilders.com/libissuesarticles.asp?id=106938

Chapter 11

[39] Water.org http://water.org/water-crisis/water-facts/water/

[40] "State of the World's Children." UNICEF. http://www.unicef.org/rightsite/sowc/pdfs/SOWC_Spec%20Ed_CRC_Main%20Report_EN_090409.pdf

[41] "Facts about Prisons and Prisoners," The Sentencing Project, July 2008. http://www.ala.org/offices/sites/ala.org.offices/files/content/olos/prison_facts.pdf

[42] National Institute of Justice http://www.nij.gov/topics/corrections/recidivism

[43] Habitat for Humanity http://www.habitat.org/how/why.aspx

[44] National Coalition Against Domestic Violence http://www.ncadv.org/files/DomesticViolenceFactSheet(National).pdf.

[45] Feeding America http://feedingamerica.org/hunger-in-america/hunger-facts.aspx

CPSIA information can be obtained
at www.ICGtesting.com
Printed in the USA
FFOW01n0118240615
14575FF